THE NORTON SERIES ON INTERPERSONAL NEUROBIOLOGY

Louis Cozolino, PhD, Series Editor
Allan N. Schore, PhD, Series Editor, 2007–2014
Daniel J. Siegel, MD, Founding Editor

The field of mental health is in a tremendously exciting period of growth and conceptual reorganization. Independent findings from a variety of scientific endeavors are converging in an interdisciplinary view of the mind and mental well-being. An interpersonal neurobiology of human development enables us to understand that the structure and function of the mind and brain are shaped by experiences, especially those involving emotional relationships.

The Norton Series on Interpersonal Neurobiology provides cutting-edge, multidisciplinary views that further our understanding of the complex neurobiology of the human mind. By drawing on a wide range of traditionally independent fields of research—such as neurobiology, genetics, memory, attachment, complex systems, anthropology, and evolutionary psychology—these texts offer mental health professionals a review and synthesis of scientific findings often inaccessible to clinicians. The books advance our understanding of human experience by finding the unity of knowledge, or consilience, that emerges with the translation of findings from numerous domains of study into a common language and conceptual framework. The series integrates the best of modern science with the healing art of psychotherapy.

T0335221

THE
DEVELOPMENT
OF A
THERAPIST

THE DEVELOPMENT OF A THERAPIST

HEALING OTHERS – HEALING SELF

LOUIS COZOLINO

W. W. NORTON & COMPANY
Independent Publishers Since 1923

Note to Readers: Standards of clinical practice and protocol change over time, and no technique or recommendation is guaranteed to be safe or effective in all circumstances. This volume is intended as a general information resource for professionals practicing in the field of psychotherapy and mental health; it is not a substitute for appropriate training, peer review, and/or clinical supervision. Neither the publisher nor the author(s) can guarantee the complete accuracy, efficacy, or appropriateness of any particular recommendation in every respect. As of press time, the URLs displayed in this book link or refer to existing sites. The publisher and author are not responsible for any content that appears on third-party websites.

For information about permission to reproduce selections from this book,
write to Permissions, W. W. Norton & Company, Inc.,
500 Fifth Avenue, New York, NY 10110

For information about special discounts for bulk purchases, please contact
W. W. Norton Special Sales at specialsales@wwnorton.com or 800-233-4830

Manufacturing by LSC Communications, Harrisonburg
Book design by Molly Heron
Production manager: Katelyn MacKenzie

Library of Congress Cataloging-in-Publication Data

Names: Cozolino, Louis J, author.
Title: The development of a therapist : healing others - healing self /
Louis Cozolino.
Description: First edition. | New York : W. W. Norton & Company, [2021] |
"A Norton professional book." | Includes bibliographical references and index.
Identifiers: LCCN 2020034470 | ISBN 9780393713954 (paperback) | ISBN
9780393713961 (epub)
Subjects: LCSH: Psychotherapy—Vocational guidance. | Psychotherapist and
patient. | Psychotherapists—Psychology.
Classification: LCC RC440.8 .C695 2021 | DDC 616.89/14023—dc23
LC record available at https://lccn.loc.gov/2020034470

W. W. Norton & Company, Inc., 500 Fifth Avenue, New York, N.Y. 10110
www.wwnorton.com

W. W. Norton & Company Ltd., 15 Carlisle Street, London W1D 3BS

1 2 3 4 5 6 7 8 9 0

*This book is dedicated to my colleagues and friends—
Chloe Drulis, Mary Meader, and Carly Samuelson—
who contributed to this work through their warmth,
support, excellent questions, and all around wisdom.*

CONTENTS

ACKNOWLEDGMENTS

I'd like to thank all the folks at W. W. Norton for their hard work, perseverance, and for making this book happen despite the challenges of the pandemic. Special thanks go to my hundreds of students and clients over the decades who have allowed me to learn the lessons contained within these pages. Finally, I'd like to thank Sue and Sam for making my life warm, loving, meaningful, and so much fun.

INTRODUCTION

*I'm not a teacher: only a fellow traveler of whom you asked
the way. I pointed ahead—ahead of myself as well as you.*

GEORGE BERNARD SHAW

After your initial sessions, the weeks and months begin to
pass, and you discover that the hundreds of hours sitting with
your clients have taught you valuable lessons. You transition
from the uncertainty of those early sessions to feeling the
early kernels of confidence. You find encouragement in the
handful of clients who have shown improvement. Hopefully,
you have yet to fall asleep during a session, call a client by the
wrong name, or forget to show up for an appointment. Sur-
prises decrease, while the number of times you can predict
what will happen next slowly rises.

As you approach your one-year anniversary, you may
notice that your weekly hours have increased, your referral
base is growing, and you're beginning to see the first glimmers of an established practice. You feel more like you have
good answers for your clients' questions and less like you're
winging it and just making things up. Your student loans come
due, and you actually find a way to pay them each month.
For some, this phase of practice represents the tapering off
of the educational process. They take the bits of information
gleaned from school, add them to unconscious biases, and call
the result an eclectic orientation. From now on, education will

consist primarily of mandatory continuing education workshops, podcasts, and pop-psychology books.

Many of us, on the other hand, can't shake the feeling that something is missing, that there is much more to learn. I questioned then (and still do) the very foundations of my knowledge and wonder if the theories and methods of psychotherapy might just be an elaborate illusion. By the time I had gotten a license and my own office, I found myself sitting alone at the end of the day fearing that I didn't know anything. Of course, I did, and you could attribute some of these feelings to insecurity or depression, but I could clearly see that the human condition, psychological problems, and mental illness were vastly more complex than I was prepared for. I wondered whether I had made a poor career choice. Maybe I should have opened a bar instead.

I told my therapist about my dilemma. She looked at me with knowing affection and told me to say more. She was a kindly older woman who saw clients in her home office. She had a beautiful view, which I couldn't imagine she earned seeing clients. I wondered where her money came from. She wore the therapist uniform of the day, many layers of well-matched colored clothes of contrasting textures, overly large jewelry, and comfortable shoes. I told her that, despite all of my education and training, I felt like a fraud and felt like I had no clue what I was doing. Being a Jungian, she interpreted this as the inevitable doubt of any heroic journey, and, of course, she was right. I felt like I was also right. My ignorance and need of continued study and exploration also seemed to be an objective reality; and reality does matter.

Flash forward about 30 years. I was giving a talk to a large group of therapists when one asked the question, "What percentage of your clients do you feel you heal?" "That's an interesting question," I said as I grabbed my chin and assumed the ponder position. "Ballpark," I replied, "perhaps 50%, those clients whom I feel I was able to give what they came to therapy for." Without missing a beat, this seasoned therapist said, "You must be a pretty bad therapist." "That may well be," I replied, "but let me ask you the same question: What percentage of clients do you think you heal?" She replied, "100%," with great confidence and a knowing nod to those around her. It had never occurred to me to think that I, or anyone, could have a perfect therapeutic success rate. Could she really be more effective than penicillin?

SMOKING YOUR OWN BANANA

I just want you to know that when we are talking about war, we are talking about peace.
GEORGE W. BUSH

As I stood at the front of the lecture hall, many things crossed my mind. It didn't seem like the time nor the place to dive into a discussion about my therapeutic abilities. The thing that stuck out to me was how open I was to the idea that I might be a bad therapist. It had taken me a long time to build up the courage to do public presentations about my ideas because I was anxious about being criticized and feared I would be overwhelmed by shame. I would have expected myself to be defensive rather than to be able to consider the possibility that I didn't know what I was doing. If I am a good therapist, what are the criteria? Who decides the measures and standards of quality? Does having a full practice for decades on the strength of word-of-mouth recommendations mean you know what you're doing, or is it possible to fool all the people all the time?

My suspicion is that the person who made the statement was somehow able to immerse herself in a theoretical orientation and drink deep and long from its particular set of beliefs.

I remembered my own fantasy, as a student, of being able to heal everyone, or at least to have a strikingly positive impact on their lives. It didn't take many weeks into my first clinical placement to discover that psychotherapy, like the rest of life, doesn't work that way. Perhaps this seemingly experienced therapist had yet to have this experience. Back in the 1960s, a rumor circulated among us hippies that if you dried and smoked banana peels, you could get the same high as smoking marijuana. Of course, this was not true, but it was funny that so many people tried it. The term "smoking your own banana" came to refer to people who create a false idea and then believe it. Perhaps this therapist was smoking her own banana, perhaps not.

I see this with my newer students who feel anxiety and shame about their lack of skill, knowledge, and clinical success. It's as if they expect to be a good therapist from day one. This leads them to accidentally erase their session tapes, misrepresent their sessions in supervision, and interpret superficial changes in their clients as significant therapeutic successes. Hiding from shame through the pursuit of perfection only strengthens our sense of isolation, hopelessness, and feeling like a fraud. The more we fake it and the more our cover-ups are accepted by indifferent or incompetent supervisors, the more fraudulent we feel. I know this from personal experience.

My own training experience was that only a third of supervisors were of any help to my development. These were clinicians who were well trained, intelligent, and compassionate, with decades of experience to draw on. The others were either poorly trained, indifferent, or were forced to supervise because it was in their job description. From what I hear from my students, this is still the case and may have gotten worse. Now that the field of mental health is dominated by diploma mills and for-profit treatment facilities, the probability of happening upon quality supervision may be even lower.

The question I am often asked by many who have gotten their license is, "Now what do I do? How do I learn to be a therapist?" I think the first part of the answer is to think of training as a lifelong process—there is always more to learn and always room for improvement. The second is to accept that having a degree and a license only represents an introduction to the field, the beginning of learning. Your challenge now is to find good clinicians and colleagues from whom you can continue to learn, develop, and grow.

SURVIVAL TIPS FOR THERAPISTS STARTING THEIR CAREERS

1. Think of training as a lifelong process.
2. Seek out colleagues and supervisors dedicated to expanding their knowledge and skills.
3. Continue to learn from experts, but avoid becoming a devotee.
4. Find the best therapist you can and stay with them.
5. Beware of smoking your own banana.

The third element is to find the best conferences, meet experts in the field, read as much as you can, and, most importantly, never succumb to the belief that you know it all and can cure 100% of your clients. Wise women and men are usually in agreement that certainty is a limited (and limiting) level of consciousness. Allow yourself to become comfortable with not knowing; approach each of your clients as an experiment in nature, and do your best to come to know them before forming conclusions. The fourth component of success as a therapist is to find the best therapist you can to see as a personal therapist who will serve as the central model for your clinical work.

Choosing the right people to learn from is the most important decision of your professional life, far more important than which school you went to or which letters you have after your name.

DEVELOPMENT AND GROWTH

Any fool can know. The point is to understand.
ALBERT EINSTEIN

In *The Making of a Therapist,* I focused primarily on the first steps to becoming a therapist—getting through our initial sessions and getting to know ourselves and our clients. There was also a focus on the fundamentals of good practice such as the importance of listening, avoiding making assumptions, and recruiting our clients into the healing process. While writing it, I was especially mindful of those things that I was told, or wish I had been told, that I found most helpful during my earliest sessions. My goal in writing that book was to walk with the new therapist, as you got comfortable sitting in the room, talking less, listening more, and acclimating to being in the therapist's chair.

My imagined reader for this book is one of the countless young therapists who have told me, "Now that I'm more comfortable being in the room, what do I do next? I ask my clients how their week went, how they feel, and whether they are working toward their goals, but I have no clear direction beyond these superficial ideas." Early on, we tend to think of therapy as a set of techniques we do to our clients. Later, we are more likely to come to see therapy as an experience we share with our clients. At the highest level, there is a shift from a need for information and control to uncertainty, exploration, and wisdom.

In the pages ahead, I will take the next steps and focus on deepening your understanding of how to use your mind, brain, and body to become a more effective therapist. I will also share with you ideas about what might be on the minds of your clients and how therapy works. In an interview shortly before his death, Philip Roth was asked about his writing process. In response, he said, "The book unfolds as I write it and reveals itself to me. I discover what it will be as it comes to life." The same is true for therapy—it is a story cowritten, moment by moment, with your clients. I believe this is the most important ingredient in the secret sauce of psychotherapy.

THE
DEVELOPMENT
OF A
THERAPIST

CHAPTER 1

SCIENCE AND POETRY

All religions, sciences, and arts are branches of the same tree.
ALBERT EINSTEIN

As long as I can remember, my thinking vacillated between the artistic and the scientific, from my heart to my mind and back again. As a student, I worried that this vacillation reflected a fear of commitment rather than innate curiosity. Successful people always seemed to be able to choose a single focus and make a career of it. My grandfather suspected that I preferred to be a student for the rest of my life; he turned out to be right. It wasn't until I read the works of the Russian neuropsychologist Alexander Luria that I discovered someone of a similar ilk who described himself as a poet-scientist. Luria managed to remain as interested in the people he treated as he was in the neuropsychology he pioneered. As the years passed, I found more such poet-scientists: E. O. Wilson, Jared Diamond, Oliver Sacks, and others, whose writings served as an ongoing intellectual and emotional ecosystem within which I found refuge.

When I think of the people I most admire, I can see that they all possess a genuine curiosity, a passion for discovery, and a disinterest in being the center of attention. They stand humbly in the shadow of both the beauty and complexity of their discoveries and love to share their passion with others. Luckily for all of us, publishers have been insightful enough to make their thoughts available to the rest of us. **The ability to be simultaneously thoughtful and emotional, to mix the poetry of human connection with a scientific mind, is the essence of a good psychotherapist.** Another such individual who would become a teacher was the psychotherapist Carl Rogers.

A CRACK IN THE WALL

> *Friendship between therapist and patients is a necessary condition in the process of therapy—necessary, but not, however, sufficient. . . . It is a means to an end.*
> IRVIN YALOM

As a young therapist, I was much enamored with a romantic view of therapy—taking deep dives, struggling with my clients' defenses, making dramatic and life-changing interpretations—the stuff of movies. I became fascinated with charismatic therapists who would direct sessions like an orchestra conductor, leading their clients to brilliant insights and quantum leaps of development. I had yet to learn that this was the world of pop psychology fueled by half-truths, unrealistic promises, and the search for profit.

It was against this background that, as a master's student, I spent a week training with Carl Rogers. My first reactions were not at all positive. In contrast to all the slick, New Age gurus I had heard present, Rogers was more of a shy Midwestern schoolteacher. He was extremely modest, wearing clothes long out of date, and so soft spoken that he was difficult to hear. He spoke of things like being nonjudgmental, authentic, and always maintaining positive regard for your client. To my ears, this sounded more like Christian dogma than a way to transform your life. Do unto others as you would have them do unto you. "How did this guy get to be so well known?" I wondered, as I listened to his teachings. I kept waiting for a punch line. Was he serious? Seeing my fellow students enraptured, I began to wonder if I was missing something. I decided to quiet the dismissing voices in my head, listen carefully, and see if he was serious; turns out, he was.

As part of our training, we had to practice Rogerian techniques in dyads with fellow students. I struggled to shift from my usual stance and keep Rogers's teachings in mind. Over and over again, I failed miserably. I just couldn't seem to quiet the river of oppressively judgmental voices in my head—of which I was the major target. I slowly discovered that by saying less and feeling more, my connection with my partner began to deepen. I was somehow able to shift my focus from labeling and solving problems to a relaxed curiosity about my client. I found that if I was able to inhibit the impulse to intervene, my client would find her own way, often in the ways I had thought of but managed to keep to myself. I also learned that when clients came to insights on their own, they were experienced more deeply and arrived at with less resistance. **The biggest insight for me as my training progressed was how difficult it was for me not to be the center of attention, not to be a fixer.** What Rogers had, that I lacked, was the courage and confidence to put ego aside and learn to make the client the center of the therapeutic work.

I came to realize that client-centered therapy had been so unappealing to me because I needed my work to be therapist centered. Not only was I working too hard, but many of my efforts were getting in the way of my clients' progress.

While my surface story was about helping others, my deeper narrative was about redeeming myself by being my clients' savior. This revelation shifted me from my previous trajectory of wanting to become like the therapists I admired to realizing that I was the one who needed therapy. All of my fantasies about being seen, adored, and admired were a defense against what I lacked—a sense of being lovable, inner safety, and positive self-regard. It was only then that I was able to begin my journey as a client.

It dawned on me a number of decades later that what I learned from Rogers was directly applicable to my more recent studies in social neuroscience. I came to see that our brains have evolved over millions of years to learn from those we care for and who care for us. I learned that the biochemistry that drives neuroplasticity evolved to be modulated by the quality of our social interactions. This means that the way we interact with others can serve as a biological switch to turn learning and brain growth on and off. Perhaps this was a primitive safety mechanism to avoid learning from those we can't trust. Then, coming back full circle, I realized that Rogers's strategies have a direct impact on the learning mechanisms of the brain. Without any knowledge of the neuroscience of learning, Rogers had discovered a way to leverage the biochemistry and epigenetics of relationships to optimize positive change. These same principles work in the nursery, the classroom, and the boardroom; brains learn in the same way across situations and throughout life. All these years later, the shy Midwesterner continues to amaze me with the sophistication of his "simplistic" insights.

If, like me, you scoff at the surface simplicity of Rogerian therapy, I urge you to give it a try. Ask yourself, who in your life has really listened to you? Who really knows you? Who really sees you? If you find it hard to think of one or more people that fit this bill, keeping Rogers at a distance might be a defense against your own feelings of isolation. Learning to do client-centered therapy isn't just managing a set of techniques; it also requires us to be aware of our own fears and needs. It is a challenge to give others what we may never have received ourselves. Rogers's fundamental insights have been rediscovered by successive generations of therapists, repackaged, and relabeled in the form of object relations, positive psychology, and intersubjectivity.

BECOMING AN AMYGDALA WHISPERER

The man who has experienced shipwreck
shudders even at a calm sea.
OVID

Regardless of the kind of therapy you practice, keep in mind that a central aspect of a therapist's job is to modulate a client's level of stress, anxiety, and arousal. The central purpose of this action lies in the reciprocal relationship between arousal and learning. Beyond a moderate level, arousal inhibits the neuroplasticity upon which memory, learning, and positive change depend. If a client is too aroused (anxious, scared, or frozen), the amygdala (the center of the brain's fear response) inhibits cortical executive networks and shuts down the biochemistry of plasticity and new learning. **The therapist's primary tool for amygdala regulation is the quality of the therapeutic relationship to regulate anxiety.**

There are some forms of therapy, flooding or implosion for example, that seek to conquer fears and phobias by overwhelming the client through massive exposure. During psychology's long and dubious history, snake-phobic people have been covered with snakes or claustrophobics shut in closets. It is now generally accepted that flooding approaches to treating trauma are more likely to deepen the trauma. Less extreme forms of this strategy have included exposing trauma victims to incremental aspects of their trauma, pairing each exposure with relaxation training (systematic desensitization). I now have enough understanding of the underlying biology of trauma and memory to agree with this position. Memory becomes flexible and changeable during states of low to moderate arousal combined with the introduction of new information or strategies (such as EMDR) that activate the orienting response to restructure memory.

Carl Rogers was a master amygdala whisperer. He built an approach around a therapeutic relationship that created a regulatory social ecosystem within which clients were free to explore their inner world without defensiveness, explanations, or shame. Our concepts of secure parenting were heavily influenced by the Rogerian approach to therapy. He helped us to realize that optimal parenting and optimal therapy share the goal of creating an optimal environment for neuroplasticity, learning, and emotional growth.

Many clients are aware of the fluctuations of their arousal and feel victimized by its extreme and seemingly random nature. "I hope I don't get anxious when I'm giving that big presentation tomorrow." Instead they might ask, "How can I lower my level of arousal in order to do my best tomorrow?" (Strategies could include no coffee, aerobic exercise in the early morning, having slides ready to go the night before, breathing and centering exercises during the 15 minutes before the meeting, etc.). I work with all of my clients to utilize and leverage the ways in which they can calm their own amygdala. Learning to be aware of one's anxiety and taming it through conscious strategies allows the gains of therapy to generalize outside of the consulting room.

THE UNTHOUGHT KNOWN

We have to wake up. We have to refuse to be a clone.

ALICE WALKER

Natural selection has shaped our brains into governments of neural systems from different eras of our evolutionary history. Some circuits are essentially the same as those in reptiles, while others are very similar to those found in rats and cats. The more recently evolved networks, those which give rise to those abilities we tend to identify with being human, are centered within the cortex. But our functioning and experience depend upon neural systems across all levels of evolution, which are woven together with one another. The limited nature of conscious processing and our narrow window of attention results in only a small fraction of neural processing being accessible to conscious awareness. This makes it easy for us to underestimate how much our brains are actually doing behind our backs.

A great deal of social information is processed below the level of conscious awareness. This is how we come to know things without knowing how we came to know them. This is also the way we come to have implicit biases and can honestly believe we are not prejudiced. Often, after something has gone wrong in the therapeutic relationship, we begin to become aware of all the indications that were ignored within our stream of consciousness. These clues, only vaguely recognized and mostly unattended to at the time, gain meaning and clarity in the rearview mirror of autobiographical memory.

Research has shown that if neural networks that organize emotional, sensory, and somatic experience are damaged, we may develop difficulties in conscious processing related to judgment, gambling, and risk taking. If you expand your notion of self to include what your brain is processing outside of awareness, it makes sense that there are always forces influencing our thoughts and decisions beyond the information we are consciously given by our senses. A therapist who is able to expand a client's awareness of these streams of information, will be able to help the client in a deeper and more sustainable way. But how do we tap into them?

We know that if these implicit neural systems can somehow be made conscious, they will not communicate in words. They will speak in images, emotions, sensations, and vague intuitions that may initially seem completely unrelated to the therapeutic narrative. Because these subtle and quiet impressions will be easily drowned out by the noise of conscious thought, we have to develop the ability to shuttle our attention between both what's occurring in the room and what's occurring in our own brains, minds, and bodies. Because nonverbal systems speak in symbols, we have to learn to listen much more carefully. Learning to read them requires balancing reason with attention to the stillness at the core of our being.

FINDING THE ALLY WITHIN YOUR CLIENT

Your friend is your needs answered.
KHALIL GIBRAN

Some clients come to therapy having discovered and nurtured a relationship with the self. This aspect of self-awareness has been called the observing ego in psychoanalysis and the Big Self in Buddhism. Self-awareness, among other things, is an exercise in imagination using external and internal experiences that allows for metacognition, or thinking about what we are thinking. When a client comes to therapy equipped with self-awareness, the therapist is able to ally themselves with this part of the client's psyche in the service of healing.

We collaborate with the client's observing self to discover ways to interpret their reflexive, self-defeating behavior and make it available to conscious awareness. If the client begins therapy without self-reflective capacity and an inner world, the therapist's first job is to educate the client about the possibility of creating one. Clients who have grown up under authoritarian control, in either their family or culture, may have neither the freedom nor support to develop an inner perspective separate from the external forces controlling them.

In some families, having an opinion that deviates from the views of authority figures is dangerous. This causes some to live in a psychic North Korea, where autonomy of thought is punished as blasphemy against the tribe, the dictator, and god. Thus, you may run into resistance driven by a client's fear of betraying those closest to them for fear of retribution in the form of violence or abandonment. I've seen this with many clients, especially in those from communal societies and communist regimes, and in victims of domestic violence. Not developing an awareness separate from that of authority figures could be a matter of life and death for many in these circumstances.

Developing an inner world requires the ability to feel safe and detach from the demands and dangers of external reality. For one reason or another, many people seem incapable of entering their own inner world. In addition to the victims of mind control described above, I've seen this in people with damage to the parietal and frontal lobes as well as in those who experience chronic and severe anxiety (which amounts to the inhibition of cortical networks necessary for self-awareness). Anxiety also increases vigilance for danger, which leads us to reflexively attend to our external environment. I point out these clients to caution you not to assume everyone has or is capable of creating an inner world.

You should assess whether a client is capable of self-reflection and has an inner world early in your work (I discuss in more detail in Chapter 7). You can use this information to guide treatment selection, the language you use, and the goals you set for your work. Many forms of treatment, such as cognitive and behavioral therapies, do not require self-reflective capacity or an inner world to be successful. Always assess the strengths and resources of your client and match their needs and abilities with the treatments most likely to be helpful. The therapy is about helping our clients, not supporting theoretical orientations.

If you see glimmers of self-reflective capacity, leveraging it to the client's advantage can be very helpful. The therapist's hidden ally, the observing self, can be trained to become your co-therapist. It is especially important because clients' self-reflective capacity can be a key component of generalizing the work of therapy into the rest of life. It is this observing part of the client's self with whom you can discuss the symptoms, thoughts, and behaviors that need to be modified. Because self-observation and strategizing for change require the participation of cortical executive systems, and because they are inhibited by arousal and anxiety, therapists need to be ever mindful of their role as an amygdala whisperer.

THE CORE OF PSYCHOTHERAPY

The quieter you become, the more you can hear.
RUMI

With its hundreds of therapies, thousands of books, and millions of words, the field of psychotherapy can seem overwhelming to the newcomer. It always helps me to remember that, when all is said and done, the core of our work centers around the fact that few of us feel confident in our basic human worth. Thus, the core of psychotherapy is to give your clients the time, care, and attention they need. **Nature has**

**provided us with a natural context for growth, integra-
tion, and mental health—emotional attunement and
secure attachment.** Yet, the need for both far outweighs the
availability of either. When I ask groups of students to recall
someone in their lives who they felt provided consistent emotional attunement, most can only recall one person, and many
sadly say, "no one." This is not to say that our clients won't also
suffer from a vast array of serious challenges, but care and
attention—the heart of the therapeutic relationship—have to
be at the center of your treatment plan.

There are notable exceptions to this general theory, such
as clients with genetic, biological, and neurodevelopmental
disorders. Many afflicted with what we call psychotic and
affective disorders may have been unable to attune with caretakers early in life and are still unable to consistently connect
with others as adults. That's not to say that they can't benefit
from attention and care; it just can't be considered to be an
answer to many of their challenges. But for the majority of our
higher-functioning clients, the lack of attunement is a core
deficit and a key to successful treatment and healing.

We are born not as individuals, but as embedded within
the context of relationships. Only later in development do we
begin to realize that we are separate from others and have to
gradually learn to also take care of ourselves. When we lose
support and regulation from others as children, we have to
replace it with something from within ourselves. Given the
proper timing and support, this can occur in a natural and
healthy way that allows us to build our inner capabilities
before external support is withdrawn. When external support
is withdrawn prematurely, abruptly, or traumatically, we are
left to take on these functions with inadequate resources that
help us get through the crisis, but often result in problems
during the years ahead. As therapists, we step into this gap
and begin the work of healing.

CHAPTER 2

THE THERAPIST'S IMAGINATION

If particulars are to have meaning, there must be universals.

PLATO

When we first begin as therapists, it takes all of our attention to stay engaged with our clients within the moment-to-moment flow of the session. As we gain experience, we discover that the bandwidth of our awareness expands, allowing us to stay connected with less mental effort. This increasing automaticity provides us with the mental space to reflect on the significance of what is happening during therapeutic interactions in real time. This is when we learn to be in the therapist's chair, not only in heart and body, but also in mind. This is when we begin to gather our thoughts, connect what we are learning from our clients with what we have learned from our studies, and address the question, "Now what do I do?"

Take for example a client who continually expresses negative self-statements, reflexively apologizes, and consistently underestimates their capabilities. At first we may simply think of these as three separate problem behaviors. But if we are able to reflect on their possible significance, we can come to see them as three manifestations of a deeper problem. This is when your theoretical orientation comes into play. If you are working from a cognitive-behavioral framework, you might see all three as evidence for a negative core belief about the self that is related to low self-esteem. A psychodynamic therapist might interpret them as evidence for the existence of a harsh superego related to early authoritarian parenting and insecure attachment. Someone working from a systems perspective might see them as reflective of the client's role in their family of origin, scapegoating, and being made into the identified patient.

These different orientations understand the same behaviors in different ways using separate vocabularies. Yet you may have also noticed that it is possible for all three to be simultaneously true. **The ability to see multiple simultaneous truths is extremely important when thinking about how to understand and treat our clients.** A large part of the answer to the question of what to do next lies in choosing the best theoretical orientation for the client. Each orientation has a theory of mental illness, mental health, and pathways to healing. Whether it is changing core beliefs, expanding conscious awareness, or altering family dynamics, the orientation you choose will provide you with a compass to chart the course and nature of treatment. The two primary problems I see in psychotherapy training today is that either therapists are trained to think only one way, or they have no solid theoretical orientation at all. The first group will have little to no flexibility in their thinking or their ability to match a client to the best treatment. The second group will flounder about, grasping at fragments of ideas and techniques, but will lack an organizing principle for their work. Both groups have their strengths, but both also have their weaknesses.

THE SECRET SAUCE

*You can't depend on your eyes when your
imagination is out of focus.*
MARK TWAIN

Regardless of the theoretical orientation you come to embrace or the type of clients you choose to work with, the one common denominator is you; the quality of the connection you establish with your client is the major determinant of positive outcome. Transference and countertransference are central to therapy, regardless of orientation. The basic human qualities of positive regard, emotional attunement, and compassion always contribute to your work. The secret sauce involves recognizing these basic principles:

- Stay centered in compassion and positive regard for your client.
- Be aware of your inner world, your strengths, and your vulnerabilities.
- Appreciate that transference always exists, and only half of it is positive.
- Remember that working with resistance isn't a hindrance to therapy, it is the heart of therapy.
- Resistance exists because it served survival at some point in the past.
- Always try to help a client get stronger before attempting to remove their resistance.

Let's apply these principles to the client who shows negative self-evaluations, reflexively apologizes, and underestimates her capabilities. The experiences and adaptations that resulted in these behaviors will also manifest in various forms of resistance. She may miss sessions because of a last-minute request from a friend who needs a favor; she may not try the experiments in living designed to bolster her self-esteem because she doesn't have the time; she may make herself ill to avoid confronting the feelings that she has suppressed since childhood. All of these can be interpreted by the therapist as resistance, and most of the time the therapist would be correct. But being right isn't helpful in itself; it has to be shaped into the correct words and presented in a way that your client can hear and benefit from. This is the central distinction between information and wisdom: wisdom is the gift of information packaged so that your client can benefit from it.

Applying the special sauce, you see that these are ways the client is trying to protect themselves from some perceived danger which they are unable to confront. Resistance means that there is more work to be done related to the resistance instead of moving on to other issues. This is why addressing content goes nowhere if there hasn't been sufficient focus on process and the resistance contained within it. In other words, resistance is not beside the point—it is the point. If this client came in complaining of depression, helplessness, and suicidality, her symptoms of low self-esteem would be the result of a set of early adaptations and defenses sapping her of her energy, vitality, and motivation, leading to the presenting problem.

When we get frustrated with a client's defenses, we are likely to blame the client for being resistant rather than taking responsibility for helping them find the safety they lack. As we therapists widen our bandwidth of observation and sensitivity, we are better able to see the interwoven nature of adaptations, defenses, thoughts, feelings, and symptoms. As they form within our minds into a coherent Gestalt, we begin to see our client's defenses as a part of the entirety of who they are, rather than a barrier keeping us from knowing them. These are the ideas, thoughts, and considerations of the rational aspects of the therapist's mind, but what about using the rest of our bodies, emotions, and imagination?

VENTURING BEYOND THE RATIONAL

*There are things known and things unknown, and
in between are the doors of perception.*

ALDOUS HUXLEY

When we focus solely on the content of the stories a client brings to the consulting room, we listen intently to their words and lock into a rational-cognitive mode of thinking. As we look for logical connections among the words we are hearing, our minds scan through alternative linear explanations, the right things to say, and strategies to be of help. The left-hemisphere regions of our brains, and the functions of mind they support, struggle to make meaning within rational frames of thought embedded within cultural frames. The left hemisphere has evolved to inhibit information and sensations processed in the right hemisphere and the body. This has allowed humans to focus on linear and rational semantic processing to the conscious exclusion of other modes of information. The downside is that if this inhibition is too strong—too consistent—it can lead us to miss valuable right-to-left and bottom-up information that is essential to knowing ourselves and others.

The fact that beginning therapists focus on semantics is not a surprise, given all the emphasis in training on asking questions, making a diagnosis, and filling out forms. The focus on rational thought is also reinforced by years of sitting in classrooms focusing on labels and theories, yet never being taught about the other channels of information available to us.

Few, if any, academic courses focus on the imagination and intuition of the therapist, leading students to believe that they are either nonexistent or unimportant. To gain access to the information communicated by a client beyond and beneath their words, we have to learn to rebalance our attention to include these quiet and sometimes coded messages from our bodies and our preconscious thoughts.

As we gain a sense of comfort and confidence sitting across from a client, having taken care of all the technical details we are responsible for, we can loosen our attention from the flow of words and begin to explore other aspects of our experience. This may feel scary at first. What if I miss something important? What if they ask me a question and I wasn't paying close attention? Therapy is about the client, so why should I pay attention to myself? While these are all valid concerns, you will discover that if you learn to trust your ability to pay attention loosely while also paying attention to your heart and your body, you will do just fine.

Remember when you first learned how to drive, and all of your attention was on the road with your hands held at 10 o'clock and 2 o'clock? As more of the basic functions of driving became habitual, you were able to relax, have a conversation, listen to music, or take one hand off the wheel. As a therapist, once you relax into sitting across from a client, you can begin to notice other things—posture, facial expression, and tone of voice, for instance. The lens through which we view our clients expands to include more and more information. At the same time, you can relax your focus on understanding and making sense of their words. You can begin to attend to your own inner world, the flow of your awareness, and your preconscious, and even tap into your own unconscious.

RELAXED CURIOSITY

The ability to observe without evaluating
is the highest form of intelligence.

JIDDHU KRISHNAMURTI

At the beginning of all therapeutic relationships, the therapist has an immense amount to learn. In fact, there is so much emotional, intellectual, and factual information to gather that it is best to just relax and stop worrying about it. Have faith that everything will reveal itself in time, and no amount of rushing will make for a better therapeutic outcome. Earlier in my career, I was careful to try not to miss anything important, which put me in a state of tense hypervigilance. I would interrupt clients in midsentence to make sure that we didn't move past something they said that might be significant. **As time has passed, I've come to realize that the really important information, the important core issues, reemerge again and again.** They are like a toy train on a circular track—sooner or later (usually sooner) they reappear. This perspective has helped me to move from vigilance to relaxed curiosity. The less you focus on facts, the more you can attend to emotional resonance with your client, which will enhance the quality of the relationship.

A safe and trusting relationship is the core of psychotherapy precisely because it provides the emotional support and regulation necessary to counterbalance the emotional and biological stressors of change. This regulation allows plasticity to stay in play so brains can actually be changed in therapy. A stance of relaxed curiosity stimulates neuroplasticity, while stress and a fear of failure inhibit it. Without neuroplasticity, there is no positive learning. This is true for any kind of learning, including learning about our clients. If we are anxious and fearful about missing an important detail or making a mistake, it's far more difficult to attune with our clients and be our most present and available selves. It also communicates to our clients that we are more interested in analyzing what they say than seeing who they are.

The challenge of successfully joining, resonating, and attuning with our clients depends upon a number of inner skills and abilities. First, we have to be our own amygdala whisperer so as to better grasp what our clients are saying, doing, and feeling. Sounds easy, but it isn't. In addition to inhibiting our right hemispheres, our left hemispheres have evolved to generate a constant flow of thoughts about the past, present, and future, what Williams James called our "stream of consciousness." It is a big challenge to quiet the mind, even a little bit, and when we forget, for just a moment, it starts up again.

I've learned through many missteps that getting to really know someone is one of life's most difficult challenges. Our brains and minds come to conclusions about others as soon as we meet them and being a therapist does not protect you from this basic human reflex. We also have to learn to attend to our own inner worlds (as well as those of our clients) in order to pick up all the nonverbal information we will receive in the form of feelings, images, and dreams. Like neurons, our brains are hubs of information and energy that reach out across the social synapse to connect us to one another. And just like neurons, brains that fire together, wire together via sights, sounds, words, and symbols, forming a new organism consisting of both client and therapist. This is the way of nature, a fundamental strategy of evolution, and it plays out during every therapeutic hour.

SHUTTLING

*Wisdom is nothing but a preparation of the soul,
a secret art of thinking, feeling, and breathing
thoughts of unity at every moment of life.*

HERMANN HESSE

In *The Making of a Therapist,* I described the concept of shuttling, and I thought it might be helpful to review it as a reminder for some and an introduction for others. Shuttling is an aspect of free-floating attention, a process of moving the focus of your awareness back and forth between your mind and your body and from yourself to your client, and then back again. Inside yourself, you are shuttling your attention between your conscious thoughts and any images, intuitions, or impressions that might emerge into awareness. Within the relationship, you are shuttling your focus between your own perspective and what you imagine your client's perspective to be—your best guess about what is going on in their internal world. Imagine this type of shuttling as going from yourself across to your client and back again. Visually, you are shuttling both up and down within yourself and back and forth between yourself and your client.

Sometimes we experience communication as coming from our clients, and other times we experience it as coming from within ourselves. The social synapse has a very wide bandwidth, in which a great deal of communication occurs outside of conscious processes. We are like radar dishes picking up information via micro-expressions, pupil dilation, blushing, posture, and who knows what else. Even though we aren't aware of them, these communications have a profound impact on our perceptions and understandings of our clients and on our inner experience when we are with them. These channels of communication that evolved long before language and self-awareness can provide us with valuable information if we both understand their origins and know how to evaluate their potential value and meaning. **Shuttling is open exploration, a journey of free-floating attention through the many dimensions of self and other within the therapeutic relationship.** Information comes in all forms, including images, physical sensations, personal memories, even boredom and distraction. Whatever you notice can then become subject to conscious consideration. It is vital to explore with an open mind and not become attached to what you find.

If someone is telling you how wonderful things are going, and you feel like crying, pay attention to your sadness. If a client is telling you how much they like you, while you feel tense and images come to mind of having a fight; if a client tells you they are sad, yet you feel anger or rage welling up inside you, these incongruities suggest you may be picking up deeper meanings. Successful therapy demands that we use our heads and hearts, minds and bodies, knowledge and instincts, all potentially valuable sources of information. Shuttling requires centeredness, calm, flexibility, and openness to contradictions.

As primates, we have evolved elaborate brain networks dedicated to interpreting the actions and intentions of others through multiple channels including body language, facial expressions, and eye contact. We have also evolved mirror neuron circuitry that allows us to detect the internal physiological, emotional, and attentional states of others as internal bodily impressions. Unfortunately, while observing and evaluating others has a long evolutionary history and complex neuroanatomy, self-awareness is a relatively recent phenomenon, less automatic and more difficult to access. This may explain not only our tendency to discover ourselves through our experience of others, but why it is sometimes unclear where we end and others begin.

As you continue to practice, you will be struck by how many times the interpretations you are offering your clients will apply to you and how often you give advice that you wish you could follow yourself. At these moments, you may have a feeling of a doubling of consciousness when you simultaneously feel like both actor (therapist) and recipient (client). Given how our brains process information, we can never know others unalloyed by our own inner worlds. Everyone we know is partly a reflection of ourselves, which makes countertransference, using the most general definition, ubiquitous in psychotherapy and in every relationship (the term "parataxic distortion" is used for this projective process in relationships outside of therapy). Given the amount of projection involved in our experience of others, it makes sense that we may unconsciously use our clients to work toward solutions to our own problems. An awareness of this back-and-forth process is necessary to benefit from our natural tendencies to see ourselves in others.

Shuttling down requires a shift in attention from thoughts to emotions and bodily states. When I shuttle down, I imagine my consciousness moving down into my chest, stomach, and throughout the muscles of my body. I relax my body as much as possible and try to become aware of any tension, tightness, or emptiness I may be feeling. I focus on and pay attention to my breathing, which helps me to feel centered in my body. Shuttling up allows you to then think through what is happening within yourself and your client, remind yourself of your case conceptualization and treatment plan, and make sense of what you are experiencing in your body. It is this oscillation among reflection and experience, feeling and thinking, physical and mental spaces that has the possibility of providing us with much richer material for our therapeutic work. Luria described his work with patients as a "romantic science," where he blended scientific knowledge and human experience. When we shuttle down, we are activating the default mode network (DMN), which processes both inner experience and our attunement with others. The fact that this same system simultaneously processes information about both self and other makes it easy to confuse the two. This is likely the neural substrate for phenomena like projection, emotional contagion, and codependence. Likewise, it is also central to the kind of attunement, compassion, and empathy necessary for intimate relationships.

Mirror neurons create sensory-motor-emotional reactions within us that reflect the internal state of the client we are sitting across from. As you become more experienced as a therapist, you get used to these intuitions and impressions emerging into consciousness. You learn how to assess their potential value and validity, and then make the conscious choice to include them in your conceptualization or share them with your client. The risk is that what you think is coming from your client may actually be from you; the reward is attunement and information that can propel the progress of therapy.

The automatic and unconscious imitation that mirror neurons allow provides a powerful learning experience through observation. We first learn from our clients by attuning with them, and later we use the same mirror neurons to teach them as they observe us. But first we have to establish a solid and trusting relationship, because the more we know and trust others, the more likely we are to reflexively imitate them. This transforms therapy into a powerful teaching tool—the better the relationship, the more open our clients become to spontaneous imitation of our words, behaviors, attitudes, and states of mind. This allows us to guide clients into states of calm or mobilization by moving to those states ourselves. Adding information from these channels of primitive, nonverbal communication to the conscious streams of information gives us a far broader perspective in our work.

As you engage in this shuttling process, always keep in mind that no matter how strong your emotions, intuitions, and ideas seem, you can never be sure if they have anything to do with your client. It is always possible that they are simply a reflection of your own experience that you are projecting onto your client. It is absolutely essential to accept that this is always a possibility. Offer your insights up in respectful ways to your clients and let them go if they are rejected. The goal is to help our clients, not prove to ourselves how smart we are. Put a pin in it and take it up with yourself after the session. If it's an insight that your client isn't ready for, keep it in mind and wait for a point in your work where it may be more easily understood, appreciated, and accepted.

PUPPY LOVE

If there are no dogs in heaven, then when
I die, I want to go where they went.
WILL ROGERS

It is estimated that 90% of the brain is involved with processing information that is already contained within the brain. This means that only 10% of our experience involves what is coming in from the outside world. For therapists, this means that much of what we experience about our client may actually be about us. The things that emerge into consciousness during therapy—seemingly random thoughts, memories, images, and emotions—can make for an interesting soup. While our client is sharing a story, we may recall that we left our car unlocked or forgot to pay the gas bill, or that it's our father's birthday next week and we need to buy him a card after work. Most likely, these specific distractions have little to do with our client, unless they reflect some challenges we are having with staying attuned to them.

Our brains are social organs that have evolved a broad bandwidth of conscious and unconscious communication across the social synapse. These neural systems within our brains are constantly receiving, processing, and sending information below our awareness that sometimes bubbles up as random and seemingly irrelevant distractions. But this isn't always the case; sometimes it may reflect a subliminal connection with our client. Don't be scared; this isn't clairvoyance. It's just our social brains doing their job.

Not too long ago I had a client who had been struggling with isolation and loneliness for many years. In recent months, his feelings of loneliness were becoming more acute and even physically painful. As I helped him become more aware of these feelings, and as he developed the ability to express them, his usual defenses were beginning to lose their effectiveness. It is often the case that becoming conscious of the defensive role of protective behaviors leads them to lose their power to keep painful feelings at bay.

As I listened to him describing his feelings of loneliness during one of our sessions, I spontaneously imagined a puppy sitting on his lap. I smiled to myself, thinking how much a puppy might help him to feel less anxious and alone. A little surprised by my imaginative abilities, I figured that this vision represented my desire to take care of him. I tried to shake it off, but the puppy kept reappearing, and something inside was urging me to suggest to him that he get a dog. The power and persistence of this image made me feel certain that it was a countertransference reaction.

Reflecting on my puppy fantasy after the session, I considered whether to bring it up to my client or not. I feared he would experience a suggestion to get a dog as minimizing the significance of his loneliness. Even worse, he might interpret it as an expression of my belief that he had no chance of having a relationship with a woman. I imagined him being offended, getting angry, and telling me off, which I would completely understand. He had never mentioned that he even liked dogs, let alone had any thought of getting one. On the other hand, I had been talking with my son about a puppy of late—I wanted to get one and he didn't. "Too much work and responsibility," he told me. Wait, who is the parent here? It was obviously not my son's desire, but my own. Somebody please get a puppy so I can play with it! This was clearly about me.

Yet the puppy kept reappearing, and my internal dialogue about my client getting a dog would not quiet down. As these thoughts played in my mind, I struggled to pay attention to what he was saying. I tried to repress the puppy image and did my best to stay attuned to his emotions, postures, and words, but it wasn't working. I guess I couldn't stand it anymore, and I said quizzically, as if it had just occurred to me, "Have you considered getting a dog?" As I was saying it, I couldn't believe the words were coming out of my mouth. My unconscious seemed out of my control! As I reproached myself with "stupid, stupid, stupid," I braced for his reprisal. What happened next left me speechless.

Instead of getting angry, his face softened and a sweet smile appeared. "I can't believe you said that! I've been thinking about getting a dog for a while now, but I was too embarrassed to bring it up because I thought you would see it as a cop-out. Even though it would be hard with my schedule and living situation, I would love to get a puppy. Even thinking about it makes me feel calm and happy." As he said this, he reached to where my imaginary dog had been sitting on his lap and began to caress it. He was petting my imaginary dog! As we talked about the opportunities and challenges in getting a dog, he thanked me for bringing it up. He didn't feel he had the courage to suggest it because it felt self-indulgent and childish. My suggestion gave him conscious permission to consider it, permission he couldn't give himself.

What actually happened during this exchange? This internal drama and my interaction with my client could have been a total coincidence. But was I picking up on something that he was somehow communicating to me? I don't believe in telepathy, but we communicate below the level of conscious awareness in many ways. Blushing, subtle facial expressions, pupil dilation, and postural shifts all send messages across the space between us that we can pick up, process, and respond to. It could have been a coincidence, but if it wasn't, I suspect that I was picking up on a range of nonverbal messages that manifested in my mind as an image of a puppy.

Even if we don't fully understand how it works, I think that therapists have to be open to the possibility that we are receiving unconscious messages from our clients (and everyone else, for that matter). Becoming consciously aware of and benefiting from these messages requires a number of skills on our part. The first is that we have to have the ability to attain a level of stillness that allows us to detach from the stream of words and our own thoughts that occur during sessions. The second is that we have to be sensitive to the subtle (and not so subtle) feelings, images, and intuitions that may bubble up into our awareness. The third is that we need to stay open to the possibility that these sometimes-irrational feelings or tangential thoughts or images might have some symbolic or direct meaning to our clients. Sometimes it might be anger, sometimes distraction, sometimes an ice cream cone, sometimes a puppy.

Fourth is that we can never assume that what bubbles up has to do with our client. Although we are not always in control (as I demonstrated), it is best to hold back and think through sharing what emerges from our own unconscious processes. Finally, it is always best to present these impressions as possibilities, and I usually add something like, "This may have more to do with me than you" as a prologue to sharing them. By presenting them as a vague possibility or even a long shot, you decrease the natural defenses we all have if someone tells us what we are experiencing. In fact, this is probably a good way to present most ideas or interpretations, even if you feel relatively sure of their accuracy.

CHAPTER 3

NAVIGATING THE
THERAPEUTIC SPACE

Nothing ever becomes real 'til it is experienced.

JOHN KEATS

Human brains are made up of a government of neural systems that extend throughout the body, somehow giving rise to our minds, consciousness, and self-awareness. While we think of ourselves as unitary beings, our consciousness is a stream of emerging sensations, emotions, memories, and thoughts. This is why our attention wanders, our memories morph and fade, and we are so vulnerable to being taken over by impulses and habits that we know are not in our best interest. Thoughts and feelings emerge and subside; clarity arrives in a flash and disappears just as quickly, and self-awareness ebbs and flows from moment to moment.

Put two people together in a relationship, and the complexity of two interacting complex systems becomes staggering. This is the primary reason why the therapeutic relationship is anything but linear and logical. We try—and we need to—to impose order and logic, create a predictable therapeutic framework, and locate what we learn about our clients in a theoretical formulation. But within these imposed parameters, the actual client-therapist process, the interpersonal neurobiological process occurring in consciousness and below, has a life of its own. Our job as therapists is to try to focus attention, our client's and our own, in ways that support the shared goals of the relationship. Often, the therapeutic process is more akin to performance art than accounting—more like kayaking down rapids than canoeing across a placid lake.

We have evolved to be haunted by the past, to focus on other people rather than ourselves, and to remember the past as we would have liked it to be. While these impulses likely served group survival in the past, they also take us away from a focus on the here and now, defending us from the uncomfortable thoughts, feelings, and sensations that need to be integrated into conscious awareness. The stories we tell can become a defense, a way to stay out of ourselves while entertaining and distracting others (especially therapists) from the cause of our distress. Newer therapists often mistake a client telling stories for an authentic engagement in the therapeutic work. **Hearing the story once may be important; repeatedly retelling the same story can serve as a defense or, worse, a form of retraumatization. When a client fills every moment of the session with words, they may serve as a wall against genuine engagement.** But how do we get our clients to talk less and say more?

TALKING LESS AND SAYING MORE

How time flies when you's doin' all the talking.
HARVEY FIERSTEIN

A rule of thumb I use to encourage my clients to talk less and say more is to guide their attention from outside the room to inside the room. In other words, if they are talking about occurrences outside of therapy, I try to find some way to redirect their focus to the emotions they may be experiencing in the present moment. If they are speaking of their dissatisfaction with someone in their lives, I may suggest that they consider how the same emotions may be present in our relationship or how they may be feeling about themselves. Another strategy is to guide clients from talking about the past and the future to a focus on the present, preferably about what is happening in therapy. If they talk about past slights or fears of the future, I again try to bring them back to the present. If I can, I try to tie these concerns back to our current interactions or central therapeutic themes.

Shifting from the there-and-then to the here-and-now poses a challenge for most everyone. Just sitting face-to-face with another person activates all sorts of anxiety related to being evaluated and shamed. This natural reaction can be amplified by an anxious temperament or by bullying or criticism from others. This is why silence can be so unnerving, and why we develop elaborate social acts that come to confuse us about who we are. As clients, we all feel more comfortable with material that we have already rehearsed and declawed of uncomfortable emotions.

Telling stories takes us out of the moment and serves to entertain and distract our therapists and us. Even traumatic stories, if told again and again, are easier to share than exploring new and potentially upsetting material. It is easy for newer therapists to confuse sharing traumatic experiences as vulnerability instead of a defensive maneuver. It is the unprocessed traumatic material that continues to impact our lives through symptoms of hyperarousal, anxiety, intrusive memories, and social disconnection.

Processing material in therapy takes many forms, but one way to think about it is as increasing the integration of conscious awareness with sensory and emotional memories associated with trauma. Processing results in increased integration of implicit memories with conscious (largely cortical) systems that allow the modulatory abilities of the cortex to regulate and inhibit their impact on our minds and bodies. Further, it allows for traumatic experiences to be located in time and space (parietal and frontal cortices), and to give them personal meaning (DMN). This neurodynamic integration is, in essence, what is happening in the brain when therapists refer to processing material.

By guiding the client to focus attention on the here and now in the context of a safe therapeutic relationship, we are encouraging a state of mind and brain that allows optimal activation, neuroplasticity, and integration across neural networks. In this safe and supportive interpersonal space, transference reactions can be expressed, observed, and processed, past experiences can be remembered in light of present realities, and our relationships with ourselves and others can be looked at from a wider perspective. These engagements reflect the activation of multiple neural systems, and the opportunity for implicit memory to integrate with conscious awareness and for experience to be combined with self-reflection. All of this takes place in a low state of defensiveness, with a brain ready to grow new connections and a mind prepared to learn new ways of being.

It is in this state of brain and mind that we realize we are no longer the terrified child of long ago and that we are having a transference reaction. All three of these examples reflect the simultaneous awareness of two or more realities. When the amygdala is active and in control, we only have one reality—defensiveness—because our other executives become inhibited. **When we feel safe, our brains are better able to hold multiple simultaneous realities that allow us to recall painful memories and integrate them with our strengths, skills, and abilities.**

CIRCULAR AWARENESS

The key to growth is the introduction of higher
dimensions of consciousness into our awareness.

LAO TZU

In order to successfully navigate everyday life, we have to maintain focus on the cause-and-effect relationships that surround us. This is the domain of frontal-parietal executive networks, the evolution of which has allowed for the rise and growth of civilization. We can understand the laws of physics, master internal combustion engines, and obey traffic rules. The evolution of these frontal-parietal networks and the control of conscious awareness by the left hemisphere allow for the successful navigation of our physical environment while shielding us from distracting input from the right hemisphere and the body.

The more primitive right hemisphere processes information in a quite different manner, likely the way both hemispheres once worked in our ancestors. Instead of relying on a focused beam of attention, the right drinks from a fire hose of parallel physical sensations, sensory impressions, and powerful emotions. We experience this style of processing each night when we dream, unrestrained by the laws of physics, the organization of time, or the constraints of civilized behavior. Old friends, still the age they were decades ago, interact with people in our current lives or those long dead, in unexpected and sometimes preposterous situations. This suspension of rules of space and time, life and death, provides an insight into how the right hemisphere functions and perhaps into the minds of our distant relatives during prehistory. While the left hemisphere processes the positive emotions of attachment, love, and protective anger, the right processes the less socially acceptable emotions of terror, shame, and rage.

During the day, right-hemisphere processing hides in the shadows, influencing our experiences in indirect and unconscious ways. As therapists, we try to encourage our clients to be more open and receptive to these subtle and often encrypted messages from the unconscious, hoping they may provide clues about the architecture of our clients' (and our own) unconscious. These messages can come as dreams, gestures, expressions, an attraction to an image, or a reaction to a song or smell. Intrusions from outside the conscious processing of the left hemisphere are referred to as intuition, intrusions, and even paranormal abilities.

FREE-FLOATING ATTENTION

*We hear only those questions for which we
are in a position to find answers.*
FRIEDRICH NIETZSCHE

Attention, by definition, usually has some specific target. We pay attention to a lecture, our children, or a sign warning us to "Mind the Gap." Some things capture our attention such as crashing dishes in a restaurant or the horn of a rapidly approaching car. We are taught to pay attention when someone is speaking to us and struggle to pay attention to those things we find boring, repetitious, or tedious. But attention is more than orienting our eyes, bodies, and minds in the direction of a particular thing or activity. Attention is also part of our perceptual system, which means that we have developed ways of paying attention to some things and not to others.

Based on our past experience, we automatically and unconsciously separate figure from ground, pulling forward what we think is important. We also distort what we see and hear based on past experience, biases, and preferences. The implicit biases of our perceptual systems do not only come to bear in the areas of interpersonal sensitivity and social justice, they also manifest within the therapeutic relationship. We focus on some things (words, ideas, and things that fit our existing frame of mind) to the exclusion of others (somatic sensations, images, feelings, and ideas that don't match our implicit assumptions).

This means that our training, culture, insecurities, psychological defenses, and prejudices all influence what we pay attention to and what it means. First impressions of our clients will more likely lead us to a search for confirmatory evidence for our initial hypotheses. This primacy bias increases the risk of missing important information that doesn't fit with our initial theories, information that could lead us to new and more meaningful understandings. This kind of confirmation bias, so thoroughly studied in social psychology, is an example of how our attention (as part of our perceptual system) selects, filters, and weighs information based on implicit schemas. This is not a character flaw, just an aspect of being a primate who has evolved to process information in this manner. We can never be free of it, but we can decrease our biases through expanded awareness.

Hindu and Buddhist monks were aware of these biases of consciousness before the dawn of Western philosophy. An aspect of what Buddhists came to call enlightenment was the ability to both see the biases and be able to see beyond them. While you and I may not be enlightened beings, we can remember that our minds are making up reality moment by moment, and that we should remain skeptical of our thoughts and feelings, especially those of which we are most convinced. It is the same skepticism that we should attempt to instill in our clients so they too can become less confident in their convictions, especially those which are detrimental to their healthy functioning.

Free-floating attention is a practice encouraged by some

forms of meditation practice. It encourages us to shift from an attachment to the thoughts and sensations that pass through our minds to observing them as they pass, and not becoming attached to them. Imagine what arises into consciousness as a river passing before your eyes. You respect its power and movement, recognize the direction of flow, but don't even consider catching or stopping it. It's the difference between being in a raft, paddling down the river, and sitting on the bank and watching it in relation to your own inner stillness. In this state of mind, expand the arc of your attention to your whole client.

Watching the river flow frees you up to pay attention to the entire therapeutic situation, including your own inner processes. This change in focus includes a shift from surface cause-and-effect connections to a greater openness to subtle impressions. It's similar to how we can look at a cloud and either name it cirrus or cumulonimbus, or apply our imaginations and think, "That part looks like a rabbit head, on a dolphin's body wearing a saddle." We suspend the requirements of logic, geometry, and biology to allow our minds to wander freely through the information. Free-floating awareness allows us to shuttle up into our minds and down into our bodies for the quieter and more subtle messages from which we can comprehend deeper meanings.

Free-floating attention is a form of playful exploration that requires a combination of imagination and a sense of safety. It can be difficult, especially for those who struggle with anxiety, to relax their vigilance. If you are anxious by nature and want to expand your window of awareness, explore ways to downregulate your arousal. A helpful technique is to develop a consistent attention and focus on your breathing. The first step is to attend to it; the second is to slow it down; and the third is to inhale and exhale more deeply. This practice will remind you that you have a body, that you are more than your thoughts, and should serve to reduce your hypervigilance to the outside world. This might sound simple, but it's not easy. **The secret to expanded consciousness is remembering to return your attention to your breathing as soon as you discover your mind has strayed.**

THE PARADOX OF RESISTANCE

I am always ready to learn, although I do not always like being taught.
WINSTON CHURCHILL

Early in their training, psychotherapists often wonder, "Why do clients go to the trouble and expense of psychotherapy if they are going to miss sessions, distract me from important issues, and not accept any of my observations or interpretations? Why does he spend the entire session talking, not letting me get a word in edgewise, and interrupt if I try to offer ideas or insights? How can she see things so clearly during sessions, only to go out and engage in the same irrational, self-destructive behavior as before?" These musings usually arise when a new therapist is feeling stuck in their work and lacks a useful case conceptualization. They are fooled by the paradox of the surface narrative—when clients come to therapy but don't see the deep narrative that makes sense of why they resist treatment. As time goes on, we eventually come to realize that the identification, analysis, and the working through of resistance is at the heart of the psychotherapeutic process.

The reason for this can be found in the evolution of the brain, the emergence of the mind, and how they develop in the context of relationships. As we grow, our brains and minds adapt to our social and physical circumstances with the express purpose of optimizing our chances of survival. This means, among other things, that we attune to those around us and learn what to feel and not to feel; what we can be aware of and what should be excluded from consciousness; and how we behave with and toward other people.

These adaptations from early in life, stored in more primitive brain networks, guide our behavior both in and out of therapy. Many of the things we may experience from our clients as resistance to treatment are direct reflections of their adaptational history. And those things we experience as defenses were likely once essential for survival. When these patterns of adaptation outlive their usefulness and limit development later in life, psychological symptoms often arise and functional behavior declines. These challenges are what usually bring clients to psychotherapy, and it is these unconscious patterns of thoughts, emotions, and behaviors that are at the core of their difficulties.

An essential part of your training as a psychotherapist is shifting from seeing resistance as an impediment to treatment to understanding it as a central focus of treatment. If we take the bait, focus on the content pushed forward, and give advice, we have shifted from practicing psychotherapy to engaging in counseling. Counseling is about all problems from small to large, while psychotherapy focuses on personality, character, and experience. Psychotherapy begins when we shift our focus from the content pushed forward to the process of the therapeutic relationship and focus on character and resistance.

The content the client brings to us is not unimportant. It helps us to understand their perspective, establish attunement and empathy, and provides essential information about their life situation. What is essential in the training of a psychotherapist is to come to recognize that our own work is based on a deeper level of organization and understanding that helps us to make sense of the problematic thoughts, feelings, and behaviors which drive the presenting problems. A

CBT therapist interprets core beliefs; an analyst interprets internal psychodynamic conflicts; and a systems therapist looks at dysfunctional family dynamics—these are all ways of conceptualizing about deep narrative and the psychological processes beneath the content.

The attempt to understand human behavior is grounded in the belief that human beings are incapable of engaging in random behavior (a belief that seems to be supported by neuroscience). The belief that all human behavior should make sense leads us to theorize about the logic driving it from below the surface. This was Freud's impetus to explore psychoanalysis and Aaron Beck's to develop CBT—both come from the same need to know and understand. All such theories posit an unconscious logic that explains behavior, and we all choose for ourselves how to understand the invisible drives of the unconscious. **Whatever theoretical framework you use as a therapist, it should contain an explanation of mental health, psychological distress, and a pathway to healing.** If it doesn't, it is probably a technique rather than a conceptualization. The roadblocks to healing, resistance being primary, should be understood within the context of your theoretical stance and specific case conceptualization.

LISTENING WITH THE THIRD EAR

There is no logical way to the discovery of these elemental laws. There is only the way of intuition, which is helped by a feeling for the order behind the appearance.
ALBERT EINSTEIN

In 1948, Theodor Reik published *Listening With the Third Ear*, in which he describes the sensitivities and inner experience of the therapist. He explored how paying attention to our barely conscious activity can provide us with potentially valuable information for our work with clients—as well as for our own growth and development. In the introduction, Reik recounts a story of bumping into Freud on the streets of Vienna, soon after he had earned his PhD. He couldn't pass up the opportunity to ask the great man for advice about his future career.

> "I can only tell you my personal experience," Freud replied. "When making a decision of minor importance, I have always found it advantageous to consider all the pros and cons. In vital matters, however, such as the choice of a mate or profession, the decision should come from the unconscious, from somewhere within ourselves. In the important decisions of our personal life, we should be governed, I think, by the deep inner needs of our nature." (Reik, 1948)

The obvious first question is, how do we access our unconscious? Pros and cons are easy, logical, and readily apparent, but how do we analyze and evaluate information from our unconscious if we are lucky enough to discover it? What are we listening for?

Let's begin with what we are not listening for—the content of the conversation, the meanings and implications of the words, the information that our clients present to us—that is supposedly at the heart of the talking cure. For the purpose of this discussion, the spoken word parallels Freud's weighing the pros and cons in issues of "minor importance." In order to get to process, we begin by shifting our focus to our experience with our clients, their defenses, coping styles, and transference—in line with Wilhelm Reich's (1945) character analysis. But listening with the third ear takes us a step farther, learning to listen to what is happening within us while we are engaging with our clients.

The third ear is obviously not a real ear, but a decision to pay attention to yourself as well as your client. This might fly in the face of some or all of your training which tells you that therapy is all about the client—a perspective that is both widely promulgated and deeply flawed. Once we make the decision to pay attention, what are we paying attention to? In a sense, we are applying the focus of character analysis to ourselves—alternately exploring our clients and ourselves. We are listening to the quiet voices deep within our experience. As Reik suggested, "We know things about a person and have no inkling of how we know them. We lack definite and cogent reasons for our knowledge" (1948, p. 272).

We need to be shifting our attention among a number of sources of information. The first category is our bodies in the form of muscle tensions, postural shifts, changes in arousal or anxiety, or the appearance of agitation. These may reflect attunement with our client's presentation or, if different, could mean we are resonating with an aspect of their unconscious that might be helpful to pay attention to. These internal states may also represent something within us that has little to do with the client and may be a function of our lives outside of the consulting room. The technique that is potentially most useful to our client would be our ability to pick up aspects of their unconscious processes in our bodies that we could bring into the therapy to explore and process. This knowledge depends on the fact that we are connected to others across the social synapse in multiple conscious and unconscious ways. Via mirror neurons and the processes of attunement and resonance they support, we can discover covert signals our clients are sending to us by paying attention to our own bodies—as if they serve as a radar dish for faint signals from distant stars. Because the message may be subtle and quiet, we need to learn to pay attention to the whispers our bodies may offer us.

A second category is any emotions we may experience, both those that resonate with the client's emotional state and, just as importantly, those that are out of tune or even contrary to those expressed by our client. When a client is saying that they feel fine, yet we feel sad when looking at them, we should be alert to the possibility that we are attuning to emotions that they are not yet able to experience or admit to. This is important data that you have to decide what to do with—Do I bring it up now? Later? Or at all? The answer to these questions lies in your conceptualization, treatment plan, and the types of strategies you choose to employ. Because your emotional reactions in session may not be about your client at all (countertransference is always occurring simultaneously with resonance with your client), you should never become attached to the idea that they are about your client. They are potentially valuable hypotheses that should be held as such, tested by you, and presented as possibilities as opposed to established truths. This is where a true partnership and collaborative mindset as fellow explorers pays off.

A third category is in the flow of your stream of consciousness. When you find yourself confused, distracted, sleepy, making mistakes, forgetting important details, thinking about your next meal, and so on, it is time to examine the potential reasons for your disengagement from your client. Of course, you could be sleep deprived or having an afternoon caffeine crisis. Even Freud said, "Sometimes a cigar is just a cigar." But if there are no external explanations, it can be very helpful to think about when you began to disconnect from your client and see if there are any clues to what might have triggered it. Another possible explanation is that part of your client's defensive system and character armor involves protecting themselves by confusing those around them. When people grow up in dangerous environments and are punished for expressing their thoughts, they learn to scramble their communications as a form of self-protection. They are simultaneously confused by the difficulties others have in understanding them. What looks like resistance may be an early adaptation that can provide information about a client's development that could be very helpful to their therapy.

On occasion, we find ourselves returning to something our client has said in passing with no apparent intention of making it a focus of discussion. Part of our consciousness follows the client into the next topic, but a piece of our attention may cling to this fragment of information. This kind of divided attention may suggest that what is sticking in our mind is a piece of the puzzle we are trying to solve. It is presented in an offhand way by the client because its significance to them has been camouflaged by their defenses and rendered irrelevant. But because you don't have the same defenses, its relevance is not lost on you—if you can resist the draw to ignore it and move on.

A fourth category would be the connection of two or more of the first three categories to see if you can develop an idea of what it might all mean. Once again, the narrative that emerges from your analysis should always be held as a hypothesis that may say more about you than your client. In fact, it will likely always be about both of you. The questions to consider for therapy concern whether something in your hypothesis might be valuable for your client as well as when and how you would use your insights.

The therapist is a guide to a client's heroic journey from adolescence to adulthood, from the past to the future, from being trapped within a web of external expectations to being the CEO of their own lives. As we work with a client and listen with the third ear, the initial focus of our early interaction gradually shifts into the background. At the same time, those thoughts, feelings, and fleeting associations that begin on the periphery begin to take on a more central importance. Clients often reflect on the fact that they came to therapy with an agenda that was organically replaced by another more essential one. They come to realize that they couldn't have seen where they are now from where they began and are often unable to predict the course of their journey. The hard facts with which they arrived have lost their substance and importance, while the soft impressions they have always suspected have become increasingly solid.

CHAPTER 4

SURFACE NARRATIVES AND DEEP NARRATIVES

Facts have a tendency to obscure the truth.
AMOS OZ

With every new class, I am faced with the challenge of teaching the difference between identifying and working with content and process in psychotherapy. This distinction goes to the core of how each of us experiences the world. We can all see the content of a session—the words, the superficial meaning of behaviors, the stated roles of therapist and client—but we differ greatly in our ability to grasp the underlying process. The process consists of what is said between the lines, the symbolic meaning of behaviors, the implicit dynamics of transference and countertransference; all that exists below the level of the information given.

Beyond the usual challenges of teaching complex concepts lies the additional obstacle of making them understandable to each individual. If I was magically able to transport my class to visit the Wizard of Oz, I imagine the class would divide into two groups: one that would stay fixated on the evil face floating in the smoke and flames, and another who would soon begin hunting around for the man behind the curtain. These distinctions, embedded in personality, biology, and perhaps even genetics, make teaching therapy a complex undertaking. How do we get those who are fixated on the Wizard to turn their attention to other things, to detach from the stimulus of the client to apply theory to the content? This challenge can be as challenging as the process of therapy itself. But there is more.

As our world becomes increasingly fast-paced and we drink information from a fire hose, our brains and minds are being shaped to stay on the surface of things, to stay in the shallow end of the pool of conscious awareness. Take, for example, the complaint of many of my younger clients and students that it takes them many hours to do an assignment that is supposed to take one. When I question them, I discover that they are simultaneously listening to music, responding to texts, and scrolling through Instagram. It doesn't occur to them that this slows their progress and leads to inferior work products because they don't remember a time when their attention wasn't divided in this way. If we take this shallow attention into the discussion of content and process, everything will seem like content. Finding the man behind the curtain takes sustained attention and active participation in the therapeutic relationship.

CONTENT AND PROCESS

What orators lack in depth, they make up for in length.
MONTESQUIEU

The content of an interaction includes the specific words and conscious meanings of what is being discussed. These are the things you would read in a transcript of a session. The process is, in essence, everything else around and beneath the words—the tone, gestures, the unconscious dynamics, possible symbolic meaning of the content, the transference, countertransference, and all of the unspoken emotions.

A parallel to content and process is the distinction between surface narratives and deep narratives. Surface narratives are the stories told and the conscious intent behind them. If you ask a young therapist, say a young woman, why she decided to pursue a career in mental health, she may say that she wants to dedicate her life to helping people. This is the surface narrative—easy to communicate, contains minimal disclosure, and is based in positive and acceptable emotions. As you get to know her, you discover that she had a sibling with a physical disability who required most of their parents' time and attention. You can see that she had to learn to take care of herself throughout childhood. Thus, a deep narrative may include that she was shaped in childhood for self-denial and taking care of others, suggesting that becoming a therapist has a deeper psychological narrative. It doesn't mean that the surface narrative is false, but it may mean that the deeper narrative holds more information relevant to the client's symptoms and struggles—for example, why they overwork themselves, neglect self-care, and find it difficult to let others help them.

Taking it to the next level, this young therapist's early experiences may have affected her self-esteem and attachment relationships in a way that only allows her to be in relationships where she is the caretaker. She may be ashamed to be vulnerable or needy in any way. This can manifest in the transference relationship as skepticism about the ability of therapy to be helpful to her, concern about the therapist's well-being, and isolating what occurs in therapy from the rest of life. Opening to this even deeper level of narrative requires greater vulnerability, openness, and self-reflection than the first two. For this client, all three levels of narrative happen to be true. The important piece to remember is that understanding both surface and deep narratives provides insight into the architecture of a client's psychic structure and more avenues of intervention. Once this particular client began to be open to her deeper motivations for becoming a therapist, she actually decided to pursue a career in art, an interest that was put aside because of the needs of her family during her childhood.

As social beings, we spend our existence within a matrix of relationships. From the moment of conception to our final breath, those around us build our brains, influence our minds, and regulate our moods and emotions. Early in life, we unconsciously absorb the thoughts and emotions of those around us through attunement, imitation, and social referencing. In the process, we form our attachment schemas, self-identity, and learn where we fit into the social order. The victories and traumas of our family, going back generations, are unwittingly woven into our psyches and labeled as truth. Because our very survival depends on fitting seamlessly into our families, we adapt to the roles to which we are assigned. Loyalty to family roles is invisible, usually unspoken, and often undetected.

Because our culture is imbued with a pervasive focus on the individual, we underestimate the profound way in which our brains, minds, bodies, and spirits are interwoven. **Even though we are aware of how much better we feel when with loving and supportive people, we are usually unaware of how their behavior alters our biochemistry, neural activation, and state of mind.** We've been raised to look inward for answers to these problems, so we only find partial answers to the question, "What's going on with me?" As therapists, we can make the same mistake when working with our clients by focusing only on symptoms, thoughts, and feelings in the context of their individual experience. This assumption of the isolated individual has been a failing of many forms of psychotherapy.

Therapists, for example, are often raised in families that don't have enough emotional nurturance to go around. We may have a narcissistic mother, alcoholic father, or a sibling requiring constant attention. There may have been difficult situations requiring that we do without the attention we required. By nature, we may also be more introverted, less assertive, and more comfortable putting the needs of others ahead of our own. In the process, we learn to be exquisitely sensitive to those around us and we find friends and partners who need the care and attention we learned to give to members of our family. The early lessons of self-denial may carry forward in the form of workaholism, poor self-care, and having a raft of dependents later in life.

We may go to therapy because of depression, exhaustion, or frustration with relationships where we never quite get as much as we give. We learn that our generosity is usually not reciprocated, which makes us feel demoralized and taken advantage of. All of the hard work that we thought would deliver us from our anxiety and sense of aloneness hasn't worked. Our therapist may make a variety of suggestions about better self-care, learning to take as well as give, and consider finding new friends. These will all sound like reasonable ideas. They are the same things we suggest to our own clients. But why can't we follow this good advice? Habit, character, and fear of change are all possible explanations. A deeper explanation may be our invisible loyalty to our families.

DEEP NARRATIVES AND FAMILY HISTORY

*It's not that I am so smart. But I stay with
the questions much longer.*
ALBERT EINSTEIN

The roles we play in our families of origin organize our brains, minds, and behaviors. For most of our evolutionary history, the survival of our tribe has been a powerful motivator. Tribes are competitive because individuals within them work together and know their role. If you are an alpha, a beta, a caretaker, a pillar of the community, or the black sheep, these roles are paired in your mind with survival. You hold onto them for dear life regardless of whether you call them character, personality, or bad habits. Over the years, I've known a number of students who were only one course away from graduation or had done everything for their doctoral degree except sitting for their final dissertation defense. Despite the fact that this final box on the long to-do list toward a very meaningful achievement easily could have been checked off, they never quite got to it.

The surface narratives of these conflicts often take the shape of "I can't find the time" or "It doesn't really matter" as ways to explain why you never got that degree. Behind these excuses, most know that something else, something deeper is going on, something tied to their role in their families. The deep narrative may be that it felt like a betrayal of your family to surpass them, or that your role in the family was not to be successful, or not to be the one who deserves positive attention. **Some families are bound together by suffering, and to break away and be happy reflects an emotional mutiny that will bring the rebel to despair and isolation.** Of course, jumping through the final hoop to get an academic degree is only one of a million examples. It could just as easily be writing the book you've thought about, asking the person you've loved from afar on a date, or showing someone the canvases you've been hiding for years.

Clients usually do not present these roadblocks to individuation as the reason for coming to therapy. They are more likely to report symptoms of anxiety, fatigue, and depression while complaining about their jobs, relationships, and a general sense of boredom and dissatisfaction. They may feel like a failure and report that those around them see them in the same light. With these clients, I try and discover what their dreams and fantasies were in childhood. What did they want to accomplish? What kind of life were they hoping to live? What did they think their legacy would be? Sometimes, their face brightens as they begin to recall a time when they were full of dreams. One client hoped to be an astronaut, another a teacher, yet another an outfielder for the St. Louis Cardinals. Tapping into this state of mind is important. I have my clients reflect on the state of mind and body that becomes activated as they reminisce. It might be too late to go into space or play for the Cardinals, but it's never too late to remember how to dream.

The barriers to pursuing your dreams usually come in the form of relationships and circumstances that arise during adolescence. Perhaps your family lacked the vision to support your dreams. Perhaps your mother was too drunk to drive you to baseball practice, or you accepted your father's disappointment with his life as the story of your own life. An interesting question to ask clients is, "If you were a success, found the love you've been looking for, or were just happy, who would be wrong?" Before asking this question, you usually have to caution them that in order for this question to be helpful, they have to name the first person that comes to their mind.

It is extremely important to remember (and assure your clients) that asking this question is not about finding out who is to blame for their problems! It is about finding the invisible loyalties embedded in the structures of the early development of the brain and making them conscious. Say your father was a brilliant man with a great deal of potential who was never able to get on track because he suffered with an addiction or attention deficit. The son's or daughter's avoidance of surpassing him will be based in loyalty inspired by early adoration, respect, and the desire to be accepted. Loyalty is a positive thing in the context of family unity, but can become negative if it comes to block individuation, achievement, and happiness.

When the emotional climate of a family contains considerable unresolved trauma, dysregulated affect, and illogical thinking, the only way for a child to join the family is by becoming part of the turmoil. This may allow them to get through adolescence, but provides a flimsy foundation for entering adulthood and building a satisfying life. Carrying their way of being to school, work, and relationships will result in discord and failure. The more idiosyncratic our families, the more idiosyncratic our brains, minds, and behaviors. I've worked with many adolescents unable to escape the gravitational pull of their families, who fail in work and school and come crashing back home.

Parents with challenges that limit their lives will often become dependent upon their children and sabotage their individuation. They may undermine their confidence, exaggerate the dangers in the world, and buy the house next door for them. It's so important that a parent develop a full life and encourage their children to individuate. The loss and despair expressed by some parents as launching approaches, and their children's expression of fear of hurting them by leaving for school, moving out of the house, or having their first serious relationship are simultaneously surface and deep narratives. One distressed father told me, "What boy could give her what I can give her?" This is a problem for both father and daughter.

Deep narratives are not limited to a client's family of origin. They can go back generations and embody the after-effects of immigration, persecution, enslavement, and genocide. I've often found that a client's symptoms make little sense in the context of their own lifetime. It is only when I begin to explore their symptoms within the context of their family history that they emerge as logical adaptations to transgenerational challenges. The last few centuries have been replete with wars, genocides, slavery, and poverty, which have left their impressions within the hearts, psyches, and genes of our ancestors and have been passed down across the generations.

It is easier to find the source of the trauma when we are given big clues, when working with the descendants of the victims of the Holocaust, the Armenian genocide, slavery, combat trauma, or childhood sexual abuse—to name but a few. It is more of a challenge when the trauma is more commonplace, less noticed by society, and normalized by the family as just a part of life. Every family has its story, and part of our job is discovering the real story, the deep narrative, and its impact on the system and our client. This is one of the reasons why I feel it's essential for every therapist to spend a significant amount of time learning how family systems work and to make this perspective a part of every case conceptualization. When all the obvious solutions fail, symptoms are most often maintained because they have a secondary gain. One of these gains is maintaining one's invisible loyalty to the family of origin.

An adolescent's rebellion may be a normal part of the individuation process, but it may also be an attempt to raise the level of stress within the home so a mother will finally leave an abusive husband. Alternatively, it may be a means of getting Father to confront Mother about her drinking. The oppositional symptoms may actually be an expression of the adolescent's role in the family, making them resistant to any intervention that is missing the real problem. It is possible that this core drama is taking place outside of the conscious awareness of the entire family.

Many people, especially children and adolescents, can play their role in the family drama with little to no awareness of the larger dynamics being played out. Because these dynamics are not allowed to be part of the family's conscious awareness, they are impossible to think about, grasp as a problem, and discuss. This is an everyday form of dissociation made possible by having multiple neural systems capable of operating separately from one another.

CLUES TO THE DEEP NARRATIVE

All learning has an emotional base.

PLATO

At the beginning of our work, we struggle to understand the words and the surface situation to come up with suggestions and solutions. If our clients are intelligent and psychologically minded, we end up telling them what they already know. The problem usually isn't a lack of knowledge of what they should do; the challenge is to figure out why they won't do it. The answers to this question usually lie in the deeper narratives. As we gain experience, it becomes increasingly easy to detect and understand the deeper narratives playing out before us. Our job as therapists is to shift to a stance of free-floating attention, loosen our hold on our client's words, and detect the other messages we are receiving.

I begin by paying attention to my breathing. After a while, I shift my awareness from my brain down into my body, the shuttling down I describe in an earlier chapter. I slow my breathing and take a few seconds to scan my body for tensions, tightness, and discomfort. This serves the purpose of helping me to detach from the flow of words and to pay more attention to all of the nonverbal information I'm getting from my clients and myself. When I look at them from this state of mind and body, I find that it is much easier to get a sense of what may be going on inside them. I get a visceral sense of their struggles, which allows me to begin to think about the deeper dramas keeping them stuck in patterns of unproductive behavior.

Working with a couple fighting about money, I might get a sense of the husband's fear of being thrown back into an impoverished childhood, the wife's anxiety about reliving her mother's resentment about her life, or a sense that money is simply a symbol of a deeper power struggle and fear of intimacy. I know these sound like complex concepts that aren't coming from my body, and you are correct. The physical input I get from being open to the deeper emotions in the room serves as a catalyst for my imagination to make connections. I'm not certain how this works, but my best guess is that when I stop attending to the surface narrative, my left hemisphere, which is responsible for such things, stands down a bit and allows my right hemisphere to find its voice through images, emotions, and physical sensations. And the right hemisphere uses images, feelings, and movement to express itself. If I can remember to listen to the messages from my right brain, I often learn valuable information about my clients and myself.

JACOB

Everything is an opportunity for me to rise.
KOBE BRYANT

Jacob was a 33-year-old man with a history of depression and insomnia dating back to childhood. He called me because he was concerned about a recent increase in his sadness, isolation, and alcohol use. When we set up our first appointment, he wanted to make sure I was aware that he was an atheist of Jewish heritage because he was concerned that that would be a problem for me. I told him that I didn't think it would pose a problem, but that we should discuss his concerns during our first meeting.

When I greeted Jacob in my waiting room a few days later, the first thing I noticed was his posture and gait. He leaned forward as he walked, as if he were struggling against a strong headwind. He approached me with a stiffness and hesitancy that made him look like he simultaneously wanted to approach and withdraw. My impression was that he seemed not so much to live in his body as to be trapped within it. Despite what appeared to be a physical hesitance, he was extremely talkative and began to speak before he was fully seated. He launched into a barrage of concerns: "I feel like I'm slowing down. I'm not doing a good job at work, and if I get fired, I'll have nothing. I sit at home feeling like I am missing out on what's happening in the world, but I don't do anything about it. My biological clock is ticking, but I don't have the energy to date. I'm afraid I'll fail at everything and end up back home with my family. Can you give me some drugs?"

The surface narrative was that Jacob was suffering from depression and was a candidate for a course of CBT and antidepressants—the most obvious diagnosis and usual course of treatment. At the same time, my intuition suggested that his depression was an expression of some deeper conflict that would be missed by reengineering his conscious thoughts. What is this sense I'm getting from the way he walks and his frozen posture as he rattles off his concerns in a pressured, almost frightened manner? Why does he speak as if he only had 60 seconds to recount his entire life? Why was he so concerned that I know that he was an atheist and of Jewish heritage before he came in to see me? His body language suggested fear of engagement, while his rapid speech reflected significant anxiety. He seemed to have an anticipation of being interrupted, or perhaps far worse. At this point, I had only these few clues about the deeper narratives I hoped to discover.

I listened carefully to all of Jacob's conscious concerns and reflected them back to make sure I was understanding him correctly. I made a list of the things he wanted to work on and showed it to him for his approval and any potential editing he might like to do. We settled on a list that included (1) be less depressed, (2) sleep more, (3) find a better job, and

(4) get a girlfriend. As we worked at this surface level, I kept in mind that I wanted to at least touch on clues to the deeper narrative before we ended our first session. With about 10 minutes left, I asked him why he wanted me to know that he was an atheist of Jewish descent. "By your name," he replied, "I figured you were probably Catholic and might not like Jews or atheists. I didn't want to see a therapist who would hate me for two reasons before we even got started." I assured him that I didn't have either of those feelings and appreciated having the opportunity to work with him.

I chose not to share that I was also an atheist and personally familiar with Jewish culture. Other than reassuring him that I didn't have the prejudices he feared, I felt that not sharing my own beliefs might allow him to project other concerns onto me that might be useful to our work. I reflexively assumed that his concerns about anti-Semitism and the rising militarism of Christian conservatives had led him to his fear of being hated by me for one or both of these reasons. I was aware that I was making an assumption here and made a note to circle back to test it in the near future. "I'm curious," I continued. "With these concerns, why didn't you seek out a Jewish therapist?" "Jews can be a real pain in the ass," Jacob said with more than a bit of sarcasm, "and I have enough of them at home." We both laughed and made an appointment for the following week.

REFLECTIONS

Development is a series of rebirths.
MARIA MONTESSORI

The quest to find the right balance of focus between the surface and deep narrative occurs with every client. On one end of the spectrum, you find clients that can't comprehend or imagine anything outside of their conscious awareness. No matter how you try to describe the unconscious or an inner world, they just give you a quizzical look and say they have no idea what you are talking about. With these clients, it's best to stay with the surface narrative, even if you can decipher the deep narrative, and work with interventions that focus on what they can see and understand. On the opposite end are clients whose day-to-day lives are a wreck but who are unable to focus on anything in front of them. They immediately retreat into their subjective world and use therapy as a way to avoid the challenges and realities of their lives. These clients need help to face whatever blocks them from loving and working in the real world.

Most clients, however, are somewhere in between these two extremes. They are aware that an unconscious exists and that a deep narrative is in play, but have few tools to discover, uncover, and decipher the mysterious forces that guide their lives. This, for me, is where the work is the most fun: developing ideas about the deep narrative and testing them through questions, clarifications, pointing out contradictions, and making the occasional interpretation. Now that I had a general idea of Jacob's concerns and goals, my next step was to assess how psychologically minded he was. By this I mean whether he was able to reflect on his own thinking, an ability some call metacognition. Put in a slightly different way, was he able to think about his thoughts, behaviors, and emotions as he might think about those of someone else? This ability to see oneself objectively provides a common platform on which the client can join the therapist in examining their experience. With many clients, it is the core of the therapeutic alliance, as you find your therapeutic ally within them.

When Jacob arrived for his next session, he seemed more depressed than the week before. The only difference was that he came in and sat in silence as opposed to launching into a monologue. After a while, I asked him whether he had the chance to reflect on anything we had discussed during our last session. He hesitated, and then said, "I felt better when I left last week, lighter, and I felt like therapy might be the answer. As the days passed, I felt worse each day than I did the day before. Now I'm wondering if therapy is right for me. Maybe it will make me worse!" A glimpse of optimism followed by increasing depression suggested to me that deep in Jacob's mind and brain, optimism was dangerous, maybe even lethal. "I'm sorry to hear you're feeling badly," I said. "Can you tell me some of the thoughts you've had this week, or any dreams you can remember?"

"Oh, this is where the therapy starts," he said with a faint smile. "Lots of hopeless feelings and thoughts that things will never work out for me. I guess that's my depression talking— wondering when I'm going to get fired, what it's going to be like growing old alone after my parents die, thoughts like that." As we sat in silence, I made a note of the fact that Jacob referenced his "depression talking," which showed that he could be self-reflective and think about his own thoughts and feelings in a somewhat objective manner. For a few sessions, I explored the array of Jacob's negative thoughts about the present and future. Through questions and mild challenges, I tried to discover their origins in early traumatic experiences, stressors during development, accidents, or physical illness. There seemed to be no through-line from his life experiences to his symptoms of depression and anxiety that I could detect. Perhaps his symptoms were purely biological and the most efficient course of treatment would be medication.

During our fourth session, Jacob seemed to be getting frustrated in his search for the source of his depression. "I think we're barking up the wrong tree, Doc," he said after a few minutes. "I think you're right!" I replied. "Let's try something a bit different. I've noticed that when I ask you questions about your family, you give short answers and then refocus back on your own experiences. I know a few details about your family but don't really have a feel for them as people or for your relationships with them. You made that offhand comment during our first session about them being a pain in the ass, but perhaps there's more going on than just that." Jacob became visibly tense and looked at me angrily. "I'm not here to dump on my parents," he shouted. "They are off-limits!"

His anger took me by surprise. I felt my body become tense in expectation of a fight. Although my first impulse was to defend myself and apologize for upsetting him, I have learned to remain silent when things like this happen. I tell myself to breathe, recenter, and think before I say anything. At a surface level, his anger at me reflected a rupture in our connection and had to be addressed. At a deeper level, I saw his anger as a defensive reflex to keep me away from deeper issues. His rage was the point of the spear of his defenses. Underneath, I anticipated fear, pain, and loss. No matter how uncomfortable I was with his rage, I had to allow these negative feelings to become part of our relationship and available for reflection. **One of the therapist's biggest challenges stay in role when our bodies and personal histories are making us want to run or steer our clients away from what we find difficult to tolerate.**

When I got the sense that both of us were calmer, I said, "I don't like the idea of dumping on your parents. This isn't a search for someone to blame. It's just that our families are such an important part of who we are that it's hard to know someone without knowing about their family history." We sat in silence for a few minutes as Jacob considered my words. Waves of emotion flashed across his face. When he finally spoke, he said, "I understand what you're saying and I agree with you. I'm sorry that I yelled at you. You're just doing your job. It just makes me crazy when I hear people blaming their parents for their own miserable lives. I just want to tell them to take responsibility for their own problems. Stop blaming your poor parents." At this point, Jacob began to cry for the first time and reached for a tissue. We had obviously touched on something, and it seemed that the rupture in our connection had been at least partially repaired.

I shifted my focus, thinking less about Jacob's hidden trauma and more about how he might be protecting his parents and family history. His parents were too young to have experienced the Holocaust, but his grandparents weren't. Could Jacob's depression and anxiety be the result of transgenerational trauma? Could this be the reason why his despair made no sense based on his individual life history? Was his concern about my religious views a piece of his family's history? After a while, Jacob's expression and posture shifted. He seemed lost in thought, and his eyes moved as if he was watching actions taking place on a screen. After a while I said, "You've been quiet," just to remind him I was there and to invite him to speak if he wished.

"I'm remembering a dream I had last night. It's one I've had my whole life. I'm dreaming that I'm in a bed covered with heavy blankets that smell like damp wool. I feel warm and safe. I have a brother sleeping next to me. I don't know his name, but somehow, I know that he's my brother. I can hear his breathing. I can feel the warmth of his body. Suddenly, there are loud noises—doors breaking, glass shattering, people screaming—someone grabs me from under the covers and throws me out the door onto an icy sidewalk. I'm in pain. Something is broken, maybe my arm. I feel someone stepping on my back, pushing me into the snow. And then I wake up."

In the weeks and months that followed, Jacob told me of his family's history and the stories he had heard as a child from his grandparents and others of their generation who were caught in the Holocaust. This recurrent dream from childhood was likely a memory he had created from those stories, about what had happened to the great uncle whose name he carried. He remembered as a child trying to avoid going to sleep so he could avoid this dream. Jacob realized (remembered?) he had come to believe that being happy was a betrayal of his family history, and being optimistic and trusting made him vulnerable to victimization. He had learned that his family who stayed behind in Europe had been optimistic about how they would be treated by the Nazis. They were unable to believe the stories they had heard and thought that good people would never let such things happen. This story was told to him as a child as a warning against being optimistic and trusting.

Although born in the United States decades later, Jacob lived in the shadows of events that shaped his psyche and haunted the dreams and memories of those closest to him. His outburst against parent blaming was not an attack against me but a protective aggression based on attachment for those he loved. Our therapeutic challenge was to somehow separate his loyalty to his ancestors from his opportunities in the present and the future. Part of his healing was to find ways to honor their suffering and sacrifice by creating a better life for himself and for his future children. This deep narrative, which became a foundation for our work, could have been missed with medication and trying to change his negative thoughts. A few years later, Jacob sent me a holiday card with a picture of his two children, a boy and a girl, named after his grandparents.

CHAPTER 5

THE MIND OF THE THERAPIST

When the mind is thinking it is talking to itself.

PLATO

Until now, we have been focusing primarily on expanding our awareness in order to be more sensitive to subtle modes of communication from our clients and within ourselves. Let us now take time to consider what we should be thinking about our thinking. In other words, we should shift from being the thinker of thoughts to being an observer of the thinker of thoughts. Some call this metacognition. We all know that our minds generate a constant stream of thoughts, associations, and opinions—some good, some not so good. The shortcomings of our thinking is a component of the fallibility of being human, therapists included.

If we try to meditate, it soon becomes clear how difficult it can be to dam our stream of consciousness, a stream that continues to flow as we sit across from our clients. Some of our thoughts apply to the client, others to us, and it can be difficult to distinguish between the two. Because our perceptions can be distorted and our logic flawed, we have to first and foremost become skeptical of the thoughts that emerge into consciousness. In the context of metacognition, we have to take a scientific approach, as much as we can, to the thoughts that emerge in relation to our clients. We have to assess them for accuracy and validity, search for more data to support them, and withhold our conclusions until we have some confidence that they will be helpful to our clients. Understanding some of the biases inherent in human information processing can be helpful to us, not only in our work as therapists, but also as human beings.

Much evidence suggests that the human mind has evolved to believe rather than coming to rational conclusions after careful observation and consideration. This human predilection toward belief was likely shaped because it decreases the anxiety of uncertainty while optimizing group coherence around shared ideas. The biased beliefs that our friends are the best of people, and that our tribe is superior to other tribes, and that God is on our side, are phenomena that have been explored and validated across multiple fields of study. These and hundreds of other built-in cognitive biases boost confidence and commitment in times of peace and war.

Our thoughts are shaped, not by the accurate assessment of data, but by selective attention to confirmatory data and selective neglect of data that conflicts with our established beliefs. This will to believe is reflected in Freud's defenses, Beck's core beliefs, and the shared myths of every culture. In fact, the power of belief is so strong that it regularly infiltrates even our best and most rigorous scientific studies. For an indepth exploration of this fascinating area of research, see Daniel Kahneman's *Thinking, Fast and Slow* (2011) and Michael Lewis's *The Undoing Project* (2017).

EGOCENTRISM AND CERTAINTY

The only certainty is that nothing is certain.
PLINY THE ELDER

You may have noticed that the distortions and false beliefs of others are quite apparent, but only if they differ from our own. When they fall beneath the shadow of our own beliefs, they magically morph from naive biases into obvious facts. This is a handicap from which all humans suffer. This means that while shared backgrounds and experiences with our clients may help us to understand them better, it can also result in missing important information that is right before our eyes. While objective analysis and hypothesis testing lead us to search for new and conflicting information, beliefs search for confirmatory information to reinforce the existing dogma.

The client in psychotherapy finds themselves at the heart of the dynamic conflict between belief and knowledge. While they come to therapy because of their symptoms and struggles, their beliefs cloak the causes of their challenges. Clients assume that the answers to their problems can be found without disturbing the fundamental beliefs upon which they have based their lives. This means that therapists are balancing between being supportive of their clients' beliefs and unconscious assumptions while strategizing about how to challenge them. This balance can create what Fritz Perls called "a safe emergency." The beliefs most central to therapy are those which lead to the creation of symptoms. In a parallel process for the therapist, those beliefs which lead to the blind spots responsible for countertransference should be the center of focus in supervision, training, and the therapist's own therapy. **At the heart of the enterprise of psychotherapy is the art of cultivating a curious skepticism about beliefs, both your client's and your own.**

A client named Sean, who is also a therapist, came to session last week concerned about what he felt to be a countertransference reaction. He had become very angry about a client's continued drinking despite his interventions, and felt that he was overly aggressive with his client. While Sean could make a rational case for his approach, his degree of emotion made him suspicious that something below the surface led him to behave in a manner incongruent with his therapeutic strategy. I had worked with him previously about paying attention to his emotions as potential indications of countertransference linked to his work. As Sean spoke about his client and the specific interactions that concerned him, I became aware of a parallel to his own addiction to marijuana.

As I listened to Sean describing the session, I could see through his facial expressions that he was simultaneously processing different streams of information. It was if he was watching two screens at the same time—one contained the shared narrative about his session, the other his personal struggles. Because of this he was distracted, his narrative fragmented, and his thoughts rendered incoherent. As he finished his story, I began the sentence, "I wonder if you see any parallels . . ." He interrupted me, saying, "I know what you are going to say," with a smile like someone caught with his hand in the cookie jar. "As I was telling you what happened, I realized that my client was activating my feeling about my own addiction, and I came down on him like I come down on myself. I wasn't being a therapist during the session. I was being the internal shaming parent that haunts me and who was scolding my client." This kind of recognition of countertransference gives the therapist the opportunity to take a step back, separate their internal conflict from their therapeutic approach, and recalibrate their thoughts and behaviors.

EVOLUTIONARY PSYCHOTHERAPY

Evolution is a light illuminating all facts,
a curve that all lives must follow.

PIERRE TEILHARD DE CHARDIN

While we rely on our brains and minds to navigate life, most of us have very little understanding of how they work—these most complex of all things do not come with an owner's manual. The fact that Sean can project his own struggles into his client and see emotions he does not realize are his own, reflects how our brains have evolved to confuse ourselves with others. Part of our job as psychotherapists is to learn how the brain works and also how to share essential information with our clients.

The first important piece of information is that the primitive amygdala was our first executive system and maintains veto power over our other executive systems. This is why, when you are anxious, frightened, or scared, you find that your judgment, problem-solving skills, and empathic abilities become impaired. We know our amygdala has been triggered when we feel bodily indications of arousal such as racing heart, sweaty palms, and muscle tension. These are signs that you should stop what you are doing, reflect on your physical and emotional state, and take time out to explore what might be making you anxious. This is a much better strategy than attempting to use your partly inhibited cortex to make important decisions or interact with others. Once you become aware of what your body is attempting to tell you, you can get your amygdala to stand down until you regain optimal cortical and executive functioning. This is like counting to 10, with the added sophistication of greater self-awareness. This is a very important skill to learn, whether you are a parent, a manager, or the CEO of a large organization. It saves you from creating the ill will engendered when the amygdala in the CEO's chair.

Knowing that you have an essentially reptilian structure at the core of your brain that regresses in the face of danger, real or imagined, can be a bit unnerving—even more so when you realize that it is a simple-minded structure that misinterprets many neutral and irrelevant things as dangerous and takes over our emotions, thoughts, and problem-solving systems. The amygdala is too primitive to have language, but we know when it is activated through the signs in our bodies. In fact, all of the symptoms of panic attacks are a direct result of the amygdala activating parts of our brain stem responsible for functions such as increased respiration, flushing, and increased heart rate. All of these activations, part of the fight-flight-freeze response, exist on a spectrum, and the more carefully you pay attention to them, the earlier warning you can have that the amygdala is exerting its executive privilege.

A second bit of vital information is a primitive socializing function we experience as shame, not about what we do, but about the deepest sense of our own personal worth. How we experience shame makes it feel deeply personal, so we search for explanations from our past to account for its existence. Early abandonment, abuse, and neglect are popular candidates around which to build a narrative to explain our shame. The first clue I found that led me away from this orientation came from the people I worked with who had intense and deep shame yet experienced none of the things normally associated with it. This led me to an evolutionary explanation for shame as an innate physiological state related to parasympathetic arousal, which makes us look to others to evaluate our worth and tell us what to do. Shame is an echo of our primitive herd mentality, which served as an ancient organizing principle of mammalian group coordination.

Put in a different way, evolution has shaped internal bio-logical mechanisms that allow us to organize groups around dominant alpha personalities by instilling in most of us the fear of social evaluation, criticism, and ostracism. This results in our always looking to others to see whether we are lovable, accepted, and fitting into the crowd. This has reached a new frenzy in the age of social media, where everything must be shared if it is to be considered real. If we feel we are not living up to the social expectations in our minds, we feel lost, worth-less, and unlovable. These elaborate states of mind are not a problem for animals with small cortices, but can become soul crushing for humans, living within complex social structures, who search for internal explanations for our emotions.

In much the same way that we need to learn to tame and domesticate the amygdala, we can also learn to tame shame. Unhooking it from realistic self-evaluation, we have to realize that we are being manipulated by primitive social forces that are not about us personally, but are far more about the mon-key troops, hyena cackles, and prairie dog coteries we evolved from. Core shame, the shame we experience about our very identity, is vestigial, much like our tailbones and the fear of spiders and snakes we continue to experience while living in urban environments. Our primitive herd mentality, combined with a large cortex, total digital access, and an amygdala that doesn't know any better, repeatedly triggers core shame through the self-other comparisons of social media.

The third piece of this evolutionary information is the fact that the lifetime development of our brains has been shaped in support of the survival of the tribe. In other words, each stage of our lives, from childhood to adolescence, the various stages of adulthood, and old age, impacts our brains, emotions, expe-riences, and behaviors to support the well-being and ultimate survival of the group. The disruptions and social challenges of adolescence, for example, have been shaped to shift us from the role of a child into the social connectivity and responsibilities of adulthood. The brain changes that occur in older people are designed to help them nurture the young, guide them into adulthood, and support tribal culture. A very important aspect of this lifetime evolutionary approach is that wisdom doesn't show up in old age without steady dedication to psychological development, openness, and vulnerability throughout life. The danger for some of us is that while old age and wisdom sometimes go together, for many, old age shows up all by itself.

The study of evolution provides us with another useful bit of information about ourselves, which is that we have evolved over millions of years to know what's on the minds of others to predict their behavior. On the other hand, self-consciousness and self-awareness are relatively recent phenomena. Because the neural circuits designed to be aware of others and ourselves are one and the same, we often confuse our thoughts and feelings with those of other people. What I mean by that is that we easily attribute (project) our thoughts and ideas onto the brains of others, and we often internalize (identification) the traits and attributes of others into ourselves. This results in both good and bad things in psychotherapy. On the one hand, it allows us to attune, sympathize, and empathize with our clients. On the other hand, it makes us vulnerable to unhelpful projection, countertransference, and enactments with our clients.

Getting back to Sean for a moment, our ability to predict what is on the minds of others, called theory of mind, evolved long before the emergence of self-reflective capacity. In fact, it is likely that self-reflection utilized theory of mind abilities, which we share with primates and other social animals, as the core of self-awareness. In other words, the existing neural structures used to think about the minds of others were turned on the self to develop the idea of self-identity. This may be one of the reasons why it is so important for therapists to be aware of our inner worlds—it allows us to use information that appears within us as potential information about our clients.

AN EXPERIMENT OF NATURE

Be kind, for everyone you meet is fighting a great battle.
IAN MACLAREN

Human beings, as meaning makers, possess an impulse to explain, categorize, and label everything we encounter. This reflects our wish to predict and control our worlds. It is not enough for us to observe something as it is; our minds spontaneously begin to spin stories about it to add context for what we are observing. An obvious example is the spontaneous gossip that is generated within (and between) us if we observe an attractive young man with a significantly older partner. The automatic associations that arise, at least in those of my generation, include "She is such a cougar" or "His credit must be messed up"—the stuff of *People* magazine and the *National Enquirer.* I've been pleased to observe that those of younger generations are attempting to correct some of these nonproductive cultural habits.

I believe that the principle of biodiversity upon which natural selection depends is an evolutionary strategy that operates at multiple levels of human behavior. Part of this belief is the conviction that each individual is a unique experiment in nature, the combination of our parents' DNA and the epigenetic processes that turn genes on and off based on our particular experiences. Despite this belief, I have a brain and mind that reflexively urge me to reduce people to diagnoses, personality types, races, genders, cultures, and generations. When I interact with clients (and everyone else for that matter), I do so at the edge of a conflict between my rational thoughts, reflexive beliefs, and cultural biases. I suspect that you are in the same boat.

I believe that we all have one of two choices. We either neglect the fact that we have unseen biases and that our views are distorted, or accept that each of our beliefs and ideas is just a hypothesis.

As I sit with a client, I am aware that what they say triggers associations to diagnoses, hypotheses, and categorizations. On good days—when I have enough sleep, food, and self-awareness—I can also observe myself making these associations and question their validity. On bad days, I'm afraid I am more vulnerable to mindlessly accepting them. Sometimes this is fine because humans do have certain similarities, and you are likely to be correct some percentage of the time using unconscious reflex. But when you are incorrect and go forward without question, you can do your clients a great disservice. Separating fact from fiction is a lifelong battle, but it is a fight worth having.

For all of these reasons, I suspect that the best way to approach your work is to consider each client as a unique experiment of nature. I believe that we should start with this idea as our baseline and that each attempt to diagnose or label be met with an internal skepticism that requires us to ask our clients and ourselves lots of questions. Instead of having the bar at the lowest level, we move it to the highest level. A low bar for diagnosis: "This was the diagnosis given by the intake worker; it was in the chart from the prior therapist; or depression was the client's initial reason for seeking therapy." All of these scenarios reflect a blind acceptance of something that you should never assume is true. Another low bar: "They remind me of my depressed aunt, a former client with the same symptoms, or [one of my personal favorites] someone like this on the show *Friends* that turned out to be depressed."

All of these things have been said by my students while discussing cases. Don't be one of them.

Always keep in mind that if a client presents with symptoms of depression, there is an infinite number of potential causes. Possibly 50 different physical illnesses, 100 different medication side effects, and 1,000 different life events, both past and present, can result in depressive symptoms. If you see your client as an experiment of nature, you will remember to engage in the due diligence required to be an excellent clinician. Don't be hypnotized by the need for rapid certainty and accept the most superficial explanation for what you see. **The value of what you bring to your clients will be reflected in your thoroughness and repeated rejection of superficial certainty.**

GRACE

You either walk inside your story and own it, or you stand outside your story and hustle for worthiness.
BRENÉ BROWN

The vulnerability needed to benefit from therapy escapes many clients. They will come in for a session or two, clearly in pain, trapped in situations of their own making. Yet, when faced with the possibility of change that requires confronting difficult emotions, they discover that they are too busy for therapy, can no longer afford it, or can't stand the traffic. There is great emphasis during therapy training on retaining clients, which means that they keep coming to see you. This is generally considered a measure of your ability to make a client feel comfortable and hints at the fact that you may be helping them. This is a pretty good measure early in training but becomes more complicated as your training continues and therapy progresses.

You will discover that the better you are at seeing your clients' difficulties and being able to lay out a clear vision of the treatment ahead, the more likely it is that those who aren't ready will become frightened and terminate. Because most serious clients will see multiple therapists over the years, it might turn out that you are number two of five, or number one of seven. In therapy, as in most relationships, timing matters. Carl Jung once said that people shouldn't enter therapy until they are 40 because until then, they are too focused on escaping the gravitational pull of their childhoods. Retention is necessary but not sufficient for good therapy, so it is not a good measure of competence after the earliest stage of your career.

Sometimes clients come to your office that may be dipping their toe into therapy because of a life crisis, occupational challenge, or the breakup of a relationship. Deeper psychological issues may be readily apparent to you but not to them. If they come in for a specific problem yet don't allow you to dig any deeper, don't consider this a failure on your part. You have done your job at this point in your client's clinical career. Keep in mind that the therapist in the next office is working with another client who may take the deep dive with you sometime in the future.

SOLVITUR AMBULANDO

The solution to the problem of walking is—walking.
OLIVER SACKS

The philosopher Spinoza famously said, "To understand something is to be delivered from it." As a young man, this was music to my overintellectualizing ears. I endeavored long and hard to understand the sources of my conflicts with the expectation of being delivered from them. What I learned, however, is that for me, Spinoza was incorrect. I discovered that under-

standing something is only an initial step on the path to deliv-
erance. I learned, in my own therapy, that "understanding is
the booby prize" and believing that knowledge of something
equals transcending it made a boob out of me. I learned that
all the understanding in the world usually didn't lead to the
change I desired, and I realized that I was trying to avoid the
anxiety of taking risks by staying in the safe intellectual tower
I had built in my mind. It was years later that I was shocked by
the clear value of the Nike ad campaign, "Just Do It."

The Greek philosopher and mathematician Zeno posed
the thought experiment of an arrow heading for its target. No
matter what the distance, that distance can always be halved
(divided by two). His question was, if this is the case, how does
the arrow ever reach the target? What is the action that tran-
scends the mathematical dilemma of the eternal division by
two and allows the arrow to reach its target? Like many of
Zeno's arguments, this was designed to highlight the limits
of abstract reasoning when navigating the real world. Similar to the paradox of the flying arrow, your analysis of all the
aspects of your client's life, the impact of childhood experiences, genetics, and temperament may never reach the goal
of healing.

When this occurs—and this is very important to
remember—psychotherapy becomes part of a client's problem
instead of a solution. The therapy itself becomes a defense
against anxiety. While the stated goal of psychotherapy is
positive change, the unconscious mission of each client is to
seduce the therapist into accepting their defenses and collud-
ing with them to avoid the frightening emotional experiences
required for change. Depending on the therapist's psychological development and the state of their monthly mortgage payments, they may be all too happy to split these atoms into
infinitely smaller particles for 10 or 20 years.

Confounding the financial and other issues of the business

of the professional therapist is the fact that it is very difficult for a therapist to help a client grow beyond the therapist's own point of development. This may lead to intellectualization and other diversions until the therapist's own therapy begins to move forward. I suspect that the majority of therapy sessions are spent engaged in circling problems without solutions, both client and therapist too ashamed to admit to the futility of their endeavor, the time and money spent, the training wasted. This is where dissonance reduction can lead both therapist and client to label the therapy a success. The ability to navigate and process anxiety, in both client and therapist, is key to successful therapy.

CHAPTER 6

THOUGHTS, BELIEFS, AND ASSUMPTIONS

Don't believe everything you think.
BYRON KATIE

It is a privilege to be a psychotherapist. It allows us to engage regularly in deep and meaningful relationships, which can be all too rare in everyday life. We provide our clients with a space where they can think, feel, and say anything without fear of judgment or negative consequences. In a well-trained therapist, a client secures an attentive listener who can reflect back what they hear in a way that helps them to better know and understand themselves.

What I've just described is ideal, but there is no ideal, just approximations of the principles we strive to attain. We have to keep in mind that, regardless of our aspirations, therapists are subject to the shortcomings, distortions, and biases of all human beings. While solid and rigorous training helps us to be aware of these tendencies, it is impossible, even for the most dedicated among us, not to fall victim to them from time to time. No matter how much we study and how many years we spend in therapy ourselves, our unconscious will always find ways to outsmart us. It is easy for all of us to confuse what we believe with what we actually know. We must be ever vigilant to the fact that our ideas are hypotheses, and remain open to being wrong, even those ideas we hold most dear.

Assumptions come in many forms, conscious and unconscious, cultural and personal, and are paired with both positive and negative emotions. We may be vaguely aware of some of our assumptions, and may even be able to discuss them openly. Research has repeatedly demonstrated that we have implicit biases related to race, gender, height, and a variety of characteristics regardless of our conscious beliefs or intentions. Although we don't experience them and say things like, "I'm color-blind," or "I don't believe in the unconscious," we have to accept the fact that we are not the masters of our brains and minds at all times. The millions of years of evolution that preceded us hold far more sway over our experience than we know.

Many of our assumptions consist of unconscious presuppositions that lead us to selectively scan for evidence that confirms them. A simple example of this occurs when a scan is given to a radiologist with a specific question. When they are asked to look for a specific problem, they often focus on the question to the exclusion of glaring pathologies they weren't looking for. This demonstrates that attention can be narrowed and reality distorted in potentially harmful ways. Research has shown that the degree of implicit racial bias one demonstrates is uncorrelated to one's conscious racial prejudices. In other words, much of how we process information is below the level of our own awareness. This is why we can thoroughly believe that our friends are the best of people, that our religion is the only true faith, and a thousand other assumptions that serve our emotional security.

LIAM

Assumptions are made and most assumptions are wrong.
ALBERT EINSTEIN

I was sitting at my desk one afternoon when Liam called to make an appointment. He had gotten my name from his physician, who suggested that he might benefit from a few sessions. I asked him some preliminary questions and found he was a 70-year-old man who worked full-time as a consultant. He had a wife, a daughter in a cardiology residency back East, and loved working in his garden. During our phone call, I reflexively assumed that, like so many clients of his age, he was struggling with depression, thoughts of retirement, and existential concerns about life's last chapters. All he could say about why he wanted to see me was that he was stuck but couldn't say how or why. I jotted down "probable depression" in my notes, and we found a time to meet later the next week.

It has been shown that doctors tend to underdiagnose and treat depression in the elderly. This appears to reflect the cultural bias that youth is good and aging is bad. Therefore, it is a normal state of being for old people to be depressed. Despite the fact that I've read this research and try to consciously counteract it, my mind reflexively went in this direction. It shaped the picture in my mind of Liam as we spoke on the phone, and even led me to jump to the conclusion of "probable depression." I share this because, **even though we may consciously know better, our implicit biases still sneak into our awareness when we relax our vigilance.** I don't think of this as a character flaw, but as a legacy of the evolution of our brains and minds. On the other hand, not questioning our assumptions is more related to education, self-awareness, and character.

Thankfully, my assumptions were immediately challenged

when I met Liam in my waiting room. He looked to be in his mid-50's, had a mane of vibrant silver hair, and was in amazing physical condition. It was clear that I had to put my assumptions aside and actually get to know him. One of the unfortunate consequences of our brain's tendency to use past experience to predict the future is that when our predictions are wrong, it is still difficult to let them go. They become a kind of default setting that springs back into place if we don't pay attention. This is why we have to remain vigilant for our ingrained biases and question our judgment and conclusions, especially when we know we are in an area of personal or cultural bias. This is especially true in our perceptions and judgments when it comes to age, gender, race, and culture.

As we settled into our seats, I made a conscious effort to clear my mind, be more sensitive to my emotions, and listen to what my body might tell me about this unique being. "A pleasure to meet you," I began, "and I look forward to getting to know you and seeing if I can be of assistance." I used these words to remind myself to pay attention and be wary of internal distortions. These words also seemed to calm him, and I noticed that he released some of the tension in his body and slouched a bit in his chair. "Please feel free to begin," I told him, "wherever you would like."

At first, he seemed confused and a bit sad. "When I see doctors," he said, "they usually bombard me with questions. I wasn't expecting this, so give me a moment." After some time in silence, he began, "A couple of years ago I realized that I had become stuck. Everything was fine with my family and work. I wasn't feeling unhappy or nervous, but I began to feel like I was living with blinders on." To encourage him to say more, I responded in an inquisitive tone, "Blinders?" "Yes, like the carriage horses wear in Central Park, so they don't get spooked by the traffic and everything going on around them.

"I have the sense that there are things around me that I'm

not aware of that I should know. It's like an intuition that I'm missing something. It's like the feeling you get when the cab comes to take you to the airport and you're sure you are forgetting something." After a brief silence, I asked, "Have you had this intuition before?" "A few times in the past," he said. "It turned out that they were mostly related to habits of thinking that kept me from being aware of something I should have seen but couldn't for some reason." He seemed to be describing an intuition about something in his "unthought known"—he felt it but couldn't put it into words or think about it directly.

Still unclear, I asked him to share a couple of examples to help me understand. After another silence, he said, "I grew up poor, frightened, and having to fight to survive. I felt insecure, unlovable, and feared ending up in the maelstrom of my family history—a tornado of ignorance and loss played out in Northern Ireland. We were all running, and there wasn't time to stop and think," he continued. "It seemed like my family and all the people we knew were still living in the shadow of famine, English oppression, and the Troubles. Like the present was the past and we still lived as if watched by malevolent guards. And when the guards were gone, we fashioned a God in their image to keep us terrified and oppressed."

I was gripped by the power and poetry of his description. I repressed my impulse to ask him about his Irish heritage, his thoughts on Joyce, other Irish authors. While I struggled to stay focused, he continued, "One way I coped was to do everything in a small way. My strategy was to stay off everyone's radar—the police, my family, and god's. If I was noticed, I feared I would be seen as rising above my station and punished. I wore blinders to stay in my place and keep my head low, like a carriage horse pulling my load. I grew up in a world where people drove drunk, had regular bar fights, and beat their wives and kids. I had a vague sense that it was wrong, but I grew up doing some of the same things. I brushed it off as just a part of being Irish. One day it dawned on me that each of these things were wrong and never did them again. Back then, I didn't realize the blinders also kept me from seeing possibilities. It wasn't until my 40s that I realized that my past only lived in my head."

I felt like I was beginning to understand what Liam meant by blinders. In my language, they related more to dissociative processes that allowed him to survive and to get along as a child and young man. They also involved early childhood learning that would be triggered by trauma or stress and reflexively acted out—like drinking, being violent, and driving drunk. Although he had clearly done a great deal of inner work to become the man he was today, it was likely that many of the stresses and traumas of his childhood remained unexplored and unresolved. He knew this intuitively, but couldn't see them clearly enough to bring them into focus. These were some of the things hiding behind his blinders.

Despite his blinders, I was impressed with Liam's sensitivity to his intuitions and his interest in exploring his inner world. Perhaps having to always read between the lines in his consulting work had honed his skills in this area. It could also be a product of his innate abilities and the dangers he needed to assess in his early environment. I now had a better sense not only of what he was struggling with but how he had confronted and successfully navigated these challenges before. So far, I had said very little, and began to wonder how much I would need to say in order to assist Liam in his journey. Perhaps the safe situation and an attentive listener would be sufficient. I could see that, although silent, Liam was thinking deeply about something and asked him if he would like to share what was on his mind.

"I'm thinking about how I spend my career supporting people with big lives, helping them to be happier and more successful. Yet, at the same time, I don't feel entitled to a big life—that's for other people. In business, I'm the best man, never the groom. I help others give birth to their dreams, build companies, bring their visions to life, but I don't feel entitled to dreams of my own." "Does it feel like you have blinders on when it comes to having your own dreams? Like you can sense them, but can't directly see or touch them?" I asked. "Something like that," Liam answered. "I resent those who live large, who create dreams and refuse to let anything get in their way. My job is to help them build their dream into their reality. And it usually works." Liam again lapsed into a thoughtful silence. I noticed that he hadn't answered my question.

"I'm wondering if it goes back to your fear of being on the radar," I said. "The people you work with seem to have no fear of being visible or attracting the attention of god or the police—they just swing for the fences. You had to get over some part of this struggle to leave Ireland, build a family, start a business, but there is still something in the way of your fully expressing yourself, of being visible." He looked very sad now, as if about to cry. "I was slammed with too much reality at too early an age to buy the dream," Liam began. "I was too sensitive. When my father told me how wonderful things were, I could see the terror in his eyes. I learned to smell fear like a guard dog, experienced his claims of happiness as attempts at self-persuasion. All I could see clearly were the tears of a drowning man.

"When I was a child, I was told in so many different ways to be humble, not expect much, and be a good boy. I think that may have all come from the trauma and fear of my family. Now it feels like they were training me to be subservient. The difference between me and the guys I work for is that they were taught that it was okay to dream. It was expected that they would be successful and that it was their job to make their dreams come true. They play to win and I play to avoid losing." Liam again lapsed into silence as we approached the end of our session.

"Our time is about over for today," I said, "but perhaps next time we can explore what it would be like for you to play to win. I'm wondering if that might be something just on the other side of the blinders." Liam absentmindedly nodded his head, obviously lost in thought. When he finally broke his silence, he said, "Generally, I find talking with people unhelpful. They share their own emotions and experience instead of listening. Usually people tell me what I should be thinking instead of putting in the effort to find out what's on my mind." After another long pause, he said, "See you next week," rose, and left my office.

REFLECTIONS ON LIAM

We make the assumption that everyone sees life the way we do.
DON MIGUEL RUIZ

William James famously referred to human awareness as a "stream of consciousness," and it does indeed seem to flow through the present moment like a stream. Our minds are always generating thoughts, never resting, even when we sleep. This is likely because they are on alert for potential danger. Part of this alert is to take small bits of information, connect them to past learning, and to quickly fill in the information we lack. What we should learn as therapists is to identify our assumptions as best we can, hold back on accepting them as truth, and be careful about if and how we choose to express them to our clients. Assumptions need to be consciously and deliberately converted into hypotheses to be tested and explored in the context of the therapeutic relationship.

Think back to my assumption, simply based on Liam's age, that he was a depressed older man struggling in the face of retirement. This cliché, certainly true for some clients, was utterly wrong in this instance. Here was a vibrant, energetic, and intelligent man who was still in the process of building his life, motivated to grow and ready to take on new challenges— the total opposite of someone trying to figure out how to stay relevant in the face of a loss of professional identity. Our brains have evolved to generate stereotypes and to search selectively for information to support them. It's not easy, but our job as therapists requires that we buck these evolutionary mandates and strive to rise above our reflexes. In retrospect, this was much more my issue than it was Liam's. In any case, the assumption was generated by my mind separate from anything having to do with my client.

Another assumption I could have made concerned his complaint of feeling stuck. When most people say they feel stuck, they are usually describing an unfulfilling job or a bad marriage that they hope to escape. Not the case with Liam— he was describing an intuition about not seeing something important that he could sense but not articulate. In this case, it was his approach to life, trying to stay off the radar and playing not to lose, instead of to win. He was at a place in his life where he was ready to see a set of deeply ingrained assumptions of his own that were limiting his accomplishments and self-expression. This is of an entirely different nature than what clients usually struggle with. Liam was ready to move on to the next set of challenges in life, not getting ready to shut them down.

Another thing that has always proven valuable in my work is paying attention to the similes and metaphors used by a client. These are often as meaningful as interests, dreams, and favorite works of art as you get to know about someone's experience and inner world. Think of metaphors and similes as images and associations from the right hemisphere that are likely communicating emotional truths of which the left hemisphere may not be completely unaware. Some of Liam's metaphors included:

- Blinders worn by the horses in Central Park
- The maelstrom of my family history
- A tornado of ignorance
- I focus on the ethereal nature of the clouds beneath their feet
- Playing not to lose

Each of these poetic images can be explored to uncover his unthought known, those things that Liam knows emotionally but that exist outside his conscious awareness—those things kept outside of his awareness by his blinders. As I brought up each of these to explore, both of us gained insight into his challenges, fears, and defenses. In some ways, his life was just beginning.

WHEN YOU CAN'T UNDERSTAND WHAT YOUR CLIENT IS SAYING

The hardest assumption to challenge is the one
you don't even know you are making.
DOUGLAS ADAMS

One of the times you are most vulnerable to making assumptions is when your client is confusing, vague, or using common words to describe uncommon experiences. As a beginning therapist, you are told, and wisely so, to listen carefully to your client's words. You learn to ask questions and seek clarification until you have confidence that you have come to some kind of shared meaning. This may sound obvious, but it isn't. As discussed at the beginning of the chapter, our brains have evolved to fill in the blanks of communication. Humans hate to not know what is going on—it makes us anxious—so our minds make things up and make us believe we've heard what we needed to hear to have the world make sense.

When I began doing therapy, my insecurities led me to believe that if I didn't understand what a client was saying, it was probably my fault. The good thing was that this belief encouraged me to keep asking questions. After testing my assumptions became a habit, another lesson awaited. Though I now grasped the value of due diligence, I still noticed that with some clients, asking questions and seeking clarification only led to more confusion. This was when I learned that **when some clients are confusing, it is actually part of an early adaptation and an ongoing interpersonal defense**. In other words, their brains and minds had been shaped to present confusing information because it was adaptive in their early life not to be understood.

I slowly began to make the connection that being confusing, ambiguous, and even contradictory could be tied to a childhood with dangerous, abusive, and authoritarian caregivers. In some families and cultures, saying the wrong thing can have dire consequences, and being clear or getting to the point runs the risk of reprisal. Research has found, for example, that children victimized by emotional abuse have deficits in the organization of the language centers of their left hemisphere. This means that the way people speak, and the effort it takes to understand them, may hold clues as to their early social, emotional, and neurological development.

One client, whose words consistently baffled me, grew up in a country with a brutal and repressive communist regime. Her parents, frightened of the outside world, were very critical and controlling, which was justified by how careful they needed to be with their words. She and her brother were taught never to speak their minds because "The walls have ears"—one of their parents' favorite sayings. My client, who possessed a strong and willful temperament, was habitually slapped across the mouth and warned that she would be taken away by the police. I believe that she had learned to speak in a kind of double talk to keep her listeners baffled and to pepper her communication with tangential and contradictory statements. A central focus during the initial phase of therapy was to help her pay attention to the logic of her speech and to keep a benevolent listener in mind who needed to understand what she was saying.

Learning to communicate in ways that allow others to understand us is one of the brain's highest accomplishments. It requires the successful development and integration of neural circuits from across the brain dedicated to cognitive, emotional, motor, and social abilities. Because the development of these neural systems is so complex, they are vulnerable to stress and neurological damage during development. Thus, the way a client communicates with you may convey potentially valuable information about their early experience, neural development, and brain health. Over decades of practice, I've learned to think about how and why clients might be difficult to understand. In other words, the content of what they say is important, but so is how they say it, and how you may have difficulty understanding it.

CHAPTER 7

THE MIND OF THE CLIENT

You can fool a lot of yourself but you can't fool the soul.
MARY OLIVER, *WINTER HOURS*

Because most clients present to us after a lifetime of interacting with physicians, they often expect that it is our job to diagnose and fix them. A medical doctor will reset your broken bone, give you antibiotics to cure your infection, and even replace a failing heart. As a patient, your job is to be passive, take medications as recommended, and adjust your behavior to support your recovery. "Don't mess up my good work!" is a common refrain from the surgeon. If someone comes to therapy with this passive attitude, and you meet it with a passive wait-and-see approach, there is a risk of long silences, unnecessary discomfort, and premature termination.

We shouldn't assume that a new client has any understanding of the therapeutic process or your particular philosophy or approach. It's important to first assess a client's past experience with therapy, their knowledge of the process, and their expectations so that you can begin therapy on common ground. A central component of socialization for psychotherapy is educating the client that it is an interactive process. Whereas physicians become impatient and sometimes resent input from their patients, psychotherapy is a collaborative process where client and therapist work together to diagnose, problem solve, and address life's challenges.

In psychotherapy, you are more like a guide or coach than a surgeon. The client not only needs to stay conscious but should be the one putting in the majority of work and effort. Your expertise will be front and center in deciphering the problem and planning a course of action, but it is the client who will engage in the experiments in living that will lead to positive change. The therapist will explain and train, but then refrain from going out into your daily life with you. You have to do the work, train your muscles, take the hits, and go through the process of trial-and-error learning. Going out on the field of life is necessary to learn how to retrain your brain and body to be unafraid and assertive, and to take control of difficult situations.

CULTIVATING SKEPTICISM

Skepticism: the mark and even the pose of the educated mind.
JOHN DEWEY

It is of central importance for a therapist to remember that our brains have evolved to believe, as opposed to objectively weighing information. As such, we believe the biases we were taught as children, those which alleviate our anxiety and make us feel certain, and those attached to the habits of our identity. For thousands of years, wise men and women have known that the source of much of our suffering is attachment to our beliefs about ourselves and the world. This is, in fact, the core principle of the teachings of Aaron Beck and the Buddha. Just beyond establishing a supportive therapeutic alliance lies the introduction of a therapeutic stance of skepticism. This translates into psychotherapy as a basic tenet: all of our thoughts represent perspectives, ideas, and beliefs that may or may not be true or useful. This is a delicate process, especially for those who are deeply committed to their view of the world, whether they be a queen, a king, or a fool.

At the beginning of therapy, I usually introduce the notion of skepticism in an oblique manner by framing the thoughts I share as hypotheses or speculations to demonstrate my own uncertainty about my ideas and to model a collaborative approach to our work. This stance also serves to model self-criticism and doubt, establishing a collaborative or exploratory stance, and to decrease potential defensive reaction to my thoughts and suggestions. I imagine it is a strategic advantage to have your client imitate a self-questioning stance rather than directly confronting them about it. If clients can learn the skills of self-reflection and question previously held beliefs, you have found an important therapeutic ally within your client.

As a caution, there are clients who, at least initially, are in something of a crisis and need to see you as the expert. If this is the case, you may decide to be more directive to help them through a specific situation. This may also be true with clients who tend to engage in black-and-white thinking. These clients may need to remain in the mindset of the traditional doctor-patient relationship for a period of time while the relationship is established. Teaching skepticism later on may or may not be appropriate, depending on their defenses, resilience, and ability to self-soothe. Not everyone is capable of metacognition (thinking about their own thinking), or seeing themselves objectively. If this is the case, trying to teach them how to be skeptical about their own thinking may be impossible. Skepticism about the self is a highly abstract concept.

Beliefs have evolved to regulate our anxiety and serve as a point of connection and coordination among members of a group. Keep in mind that if you successfully challenge a belief, you are taking away something that the client has used for emotional regulation and a sense of safety. The goal is not to slap them with reality, but to guide them to self-observation while providing some of the emotional scaffolding they lose when their core beliefs are threatened. We become the support they lack by staying engaged long enough to become part of their memory, awareness, and self-reflection.

THE HAUNTING

I myself have suffered periodically from hearing voices at night when I'm trying to sleep.
ELIZABETH GEORGE

The idea that I may be haunting my clients occurred to me after so many told me that they "heard my voice" when on the horns of a dilemma or confronted with a challenging situation. They recall our conversations, ask themselves, "What would Lou do?" and come back to sessions saying, "You're going to be proud of me!" Learning through relationships is probably the most primitive and time-honored strategy for the transmission of knowledge from one person to another. This happens with parents, teachers, heroes, and other meaningful people in our lives. In my work as a corporate coach, struggling executives will imitate successful CEOs when developing strategy or making presentations. We often underestimate the power of modeling behaviors, attitudes, and beliefs because it occurs unconsciously within the matrix of others. People watch and absorb who we are—our words carry far less weight than our actions. Parents who tell their children, "Do what I say, not what I do," are fighting a losing battle.

When anyone is faced with an important situation, their brains and minds will trigger and even recall relevant past experience they need to bring to bear. If a 14-year-old is offered some weed on the school bus, his reaction is going to depend on a range of factors. If he is anxious because he spent the night worrying about whether his parents would come home from a drinking binge, he might respond one way. If his mind is full of the information he and his mom have been going over for the last two days in preparation for his history test, he might respond in another. The first boy may not possess an internal model of a parent who is a source of security, or see himself as worthy of pride. The second boy's first thought might be how it would break his mother's heart if he got high, failed the test, or got busted. The ability to see and feel her pain in his mind's eye and throughout his body could affect his choice. We use memory, in the form of stories, visual images, and emotions, to remind and guide us in our behavior. Our memories serve as the mind's blueprints for action and decision making.

People often come to therapy because they are doing something they shouldn't or because they aren't doing something they should. In either case, they come to a point where an ingrained behavioral pattern gets activated, and they reflexively repeat what is familiar to them. On the one hand, she takes the first drink, knowing that it will lead to the next 10. On the other, he turns down the offer of a promotion because "it's not the right time." These folks might come to therapy self-labeled as suffering from alcoholism and fear of success. They might have a vague idea about the past experiences and emotions connected to their symptoms and a list of past attempts to change. They both have a challenge of inhibition—she, to inhibit the initial behavior that leads to a self-destructive binge; he, to inhibit whatever fear causes him to back away from the promotion.

What we do in therapy most of the time is to stimulate and activate the cortex by talking about the challenge to enhance awareness and understanding. This builds an expanding network of associations and connections, both in the mind and in the wetware of the brain, that increases cortical activation and executive functioning. When cortical activation reaches critical mass, the reflexes no longer have sole control of our behavior, and we come to be able to think about what we are doing and make different choices. Although up until this point we don't really possess free will, when we are able to add conscious thought to the equation, we have the freedom to engage in free won't. With conscious awareness and participation of executive cortical systems, there is an option to say no to the drink and no to shrinking from a challenge.

BUILDING AN INNER WORLD

Happy people build their inner world.
Unhappy people blame their outer world.
ANONYMOUS

An inner world is an imaginary place we can retreat to for reflection, comfort, and a break from the concerns of everyday life. It is a place outside of time and space, apart from social conformity and from the concerns of moment-to-moment survival. It includes an awareness of our bodies, emotions, and memories. I remember as a young child how much I enjoyed lying in the grass under a tree and watching the sun and the clouds pass through the branches. I wondered if what I was observing was the sky moving across the earth or the earth spinning under the sky. I pondered the universe, imagined life on other planets, and wondered what it would be like to be an astronaut. These and a million other thoughts, which no one around me appeared to be interested in, filled my idle hours. The more time I spent in my inner world, the more elaborate and interesting it became, and the more it became part of my everyday life. It helped me to remember who I was, make my own decisions, and think about the future. It also gave me a place to go when I was sad or upset about something and needed time to think.

As someone who developed an inner world relatively early in life, I took it for granted that everyone had a similar place within them. I was well into my 30s when I began to realize that many people didn't possess an inner world. This was especially true for clients who had extreme difficulties with self-soothing. I came to realize that without an internal world, we are totally reliant on material objects, ideologies, and those around us for our very identity. This helped me to understand more deeply why people cling to abusive relationships, can be so vulnerable to addictions, and place so much stock in social comparisons of wealth, power, and celebrity.

It is clear that attachment to others, navigating the physical world, and having a theory of mind of others are all ancient abilities we share with our primate relatives. In contrast, the creation of an inner world appears to be a relatively new evolutionary development. Self-awareness and building an inner world are abilities we have to discover, build, and nurture over time. The people I meet who lack the experience of an inner world tend to have grown up around others who lacked self-reflection. Perhaps they had a narcissistic parent or considerable family stress that led to a sole focus on external survival. An important part of developing an inner world may be having at least one person in your life who is curious about what you think and feel. I was lucky as a child to be surrounded by a number of adults who enjoyed spending time and talking with me and were interested in my ideas and opinions.

Still others, having survived great hardships such as child abuse, war, and genocide, live in a state of exile from themselves. They stay vigilantly focused on the outside world, constantly keeping an eye out for danger. Asking them to close their eyes and clear their minds fills them with anxiety and dread. And if they are able to turn away from external distractions and look inward, they are instantly overwhelmed by what they see. As one of my clients told me, "When I look inside, all I see is blood and broken glass." These folks maintain a kind of manic defense that keeps them ever busy and distracted from their thoughts and a step ahead of their feelings. Like most, I took my early years of safety for granted, but many are not so lucky and have to remain ever vigilant for external threats and internal demons.

An inner world is something we create and develop over many years. It assumes adequate care and physical safety and requires being cared for by those who are curious about what we are thinking, feeling, and experiencing. We often see that the children of narcissistic parents enter adulthood with little sense of self but an elaborate sense of others.

Instead of being mirrored by their parents and learning about themselves, they attend to their parents' needs and see the world (and themselves) through their parents' eyes; and later in life, through the eyes of others. This is shaped by caretakers who have no curiosity about their child but instead see them as extensions of their own needs. I have had clients raised in Germany under the child-rearing guidelines of the Nazis, whose techniques were designed to keep children from developing a sense of a separate self so as to become better tools of the party. Clients raised in collectivist cultures will easily confuse an inner world with selfishness and a lack of respect for others. Thus, an inner world can go undeveloped due to neglect, a totally outer focus, self-centered caretakers, and a number of other reasons.

All of this suggests that, as therapists, **we should not assume that a client has an inner world, a sense of self, or even defined personal boundaries.** Because the self is an imaginary construct, it can be formed in any way that is best adapted to survive within the family of origin. For many clients, therapy may be the first relationship that has allowed them the space and safety to reflect on themselves and create a sense of self.

You can assess if a client has an internal world by what they say and don't say about themselves, their relationships, and their daily experiences. Those who live outside of themselves have only externally biased motivations and concerns and don't address subjective experience when describing their relationships and careers. I'll often ask clients what they are thinking about when they are silent during a session, or ask them a question like, "When you're alone on a quiet Sunday afternoon, what thoughts cross your mind?" If they say something like "That never happens," I usually press a bit and ask the same question in a few different ways. If you ask a client if they have ever taken a trip by themselves and they respond with, "Why would I do a stupid thing like that?," you may get the sense that they have to stay active, distracted, and engaged to avoid becoming anxious, depressed, or worse. These folks often lack an inner world and the capacity to be alone.

If you come to realize that a client seems devoid of subjectivity and lacks an internal world, and you think having one might be helpful, you may want to try and help them build one. I usually start with some kind of focused body work to increase somatic awareness. I'll ask them to imagine moving their consciousness to different points in the body and become aware of any muscle tension, sensations, or feelings associated with each particular spot. This can help to build an imaginal three-dimensional space within them. I'll then work with them to build a space, perhaps a comfortable room, that they can furnish to their taste. This will be a safe internal space to retreat to when needed. Whether this proves helpful depends upon their ability to manage the stress it will cause, their imaginal abilities, and your creativity.

Building an internal world doesn't have to be deadly serious; some humor and play may ease some of the stress. Perhaps they can imagine being at the top of a Ferris wheel or on a sailboat floating on a calm lake. Perhaps they may even want you to join them for a visit. It can be in the woods, on an island, or on the moon as a start and can always be moved if your client realizes that they would rather be on a beach under the tropical sun. The important thing is that they create some imaginary place where they feel safe and can begin to explore their feelings, thoughts, and bodily states. It is also a good idea to return to this safe place each session and suggest that your client visit daily between sessions to make it increasingly real and available to them.

Clients who don't have a sense of self usually experience crushing shame that they attempt to control through perfectionism or obliterate via distractions, compulsions, and addictions. They are often unaware of how they feel about things, what they like, or what they care to do. They have learned not to have an opinion, be assertive, or leave a mark of any kind. Self-reflective capacity and an inner world are a complex evolutionary and developmental accomplishment. They require a theory of mind, an awareness of one's emotional and somatic state, and the ability to see ourselves as others might—a kind of self-objectification. It also relies on our ability to regulate our emotions enough to tolerate seeing ourselves without the filters and defenses that calm our anxieties. These abilities can all contribute to becoming self-possessed and self-aware, and the CEOs of our lives.

WHEN LESS IS MORE

Simplicity is the ultimate form of sophistication.

LEONARDO DA VINCI

Newer therapists are understandably insecure about their knowledge and capabilities (a far superior place to begin than false certainty). They tend to measure themselves by how facile they are with technical details related to issues of diagnosis and treatment, a holdover from the classroom. **On the other hand, newer therapists seldom realize how much they have to offer their clients just by being human.** Given that therapists, like other humans, struggle with feelings of core shame, they tend to undervalue themselves as people and focus on the need to come up with intelligent-sounding answers. This leads to a lack of authenticity in the therapeutic relationship and can turn it into an intellectual discussion rather than an emotionally healing connection.

Always keep in mind that being in the role of the therapist lends credibility, whether deserved or not. In addition, the simple fact that you are not your client means you have a perspective on them which they lack. During early sessions with most of my clients, I don't usually offer any interpretations, suggestions, or advice. I simply create a safe space in which I stay still and calm while listening intently. I want to hear what they have to say, understand their feelings, and ultimately help them to feel seen, felt, and heard. The skills I employ are focused attention, a desire to understand their experience, and remembering to ask lots of questions and not to make assumptions. My ignorance and curiosity allow for the opportunity to reflect on experiences in the presence of an interested observer.

When he was around 11, my son asked me to help him with his homework. This was something he usually asked his mom to do, so I felt happy to be asked. I found a chair, pulled it up alongside him, and started to look over what he was working on. A scatter of papers surrounded his computer, and he seemed to already be underway on the task. I looked around to see if I could spot anything that I could help with, and noticed a couple of spelling errors on the screen. "Excuse me, Hon," I said, and, pointing to the screen, I told him I could see a couple of words he needed to correct. "Dad!" he said. "I'm concentrating!" and dismissed my input. I felt a bit hurt, but I sat with my feelings and waited for him to ask for help.

After a few minutes, he described to me what he was working on and the trouble he was having coming up with a way of connecting two different parts of a story. As he started telling me the stories, I tried to make a suggestion, but he shushed me and said he was trying to think. "Do you really want me to help you?" I asked. "Yes, just don't talk." Again, my feelings were hurt and I got up to leave. As I stood up, he said, "Where are you going?" "I've got things to do," I said, "and you don't really need my help." I left the room, over his protests, and went to lick my wounds. Why did he ask me to help him and then not let me help him? Was I missing something?

I went back in and said that I was sorry that I left and that I would like to help him, and once again sat down next to him. This time, instead of looking at his work, I sat back, kept quiet, and observed. Every so often, he would tell me an idea he thought of or a connection he had just made. I'd compliment him, rub his back, and say "Good job." This went on for about an hour until he announced, "We're finished!"

"Great," I said. "How about we relax a bit and watch TV or play a game?" We went, got a snack, and hunkered down to watch a show. As we waited for it to begin, I asked him if I had been of help with his homework. He looked at me quizzically and said, "You were great!" He had taught me what he needed me to do, and I was eventually able to figure it out. The best

I can make of it is that he needed my company, perhaps for emotional regulation that I didn't realize he needed. I recalled that when he was very small, he loved to watch *Peter Pan*, and would wait for the arrival of Captain Hook and an alligator who had swallowed a clock. Right before either arrived on the screen, he would scramble behind me and surround himself with pillows.

Once I turned around to say something to him, and he looked terrified! He trembled, his mouth hung open, and he was moving his hands toward one another as if to clap, but never touching them together. I felt an immediate rush of protectiveness and got in front of him to block the screen. He let out a scream and climbed over me so he could see Hook. He was riveted to the screen. I was amazed that he didn't want me to keep him from Hook—he just wanted me to be there if things got out of hand. Perhaps homework was the same; not scary enough to make him tremble, but anxiety-provoking enough to benefit from having his safe haven close at hand. When he asked for my help, he was really asking for my presence. It's not easy raising a father, but he's figuring it out.

CHAPTER 8

THE MIND IN THE BODY

*Every muscular rigidity contains the history
and the meaning of its origin.*

WILHELM REICH

In my previous book, *The Making of a Therapist*, I briefly alluded to Wilhelm Reich and his thoughts about how to think about and work with resistance. I held off discussing these ideas in detail because they are a bit too complex for beginning therapists. But the time has come. Wilhelm Reich was a physician and psychoanalyst who directed Sigmund Freud's clinic in Vienna during the 1920s. He gradually developed his own analytic theories about the defenses and eventually split with Freud over their differences. Despite the split with her father, his theories heavily influenced Anna Freud's classic work, *The Ego and the Mechanisms of Defense* (1936).

Reich's theories and techniques about how defenses are held in the body served as a foundation for the development of psychotherapeutic massage called Rolfing, Gestalt therapy, and many of the current somatic psychotherapies. Although Reich's thinking was highly influential in the history of psychotherapy, he was pushed from the mainstream because his teachings were considered radical, overly sexualized, and politically unpopular. The story of his life is fascinating and far too complex to discuss here, but if you are interested, I encourage you to read his biography *Fury on Earth* by Myron Sharaf. The focus here is his basic theory of character analysis, which is described in detail in the first half of Reich's book of the same name.

EMBODIED EMOTIONAL DEFENSES

Think of body-mind as a field of information and energy. . . .
Then realize that emotions are everywhere in the body.
CANDACE PERTH

Reich looked beyond the spoken word to a focus on a client's body and behavior. He described how physical movements, postures, and interpersonal attitudes can embody painful experiences and the defenses established against them. Because of this, he urged us to learn how to interpret a client's bearing, mannerisms, and gestures within the transference relationship. He saw them as expressions of the defenses that keep them safe while limiting their growth and development. While adults may not consciously remember what happened to them or how they coped with stress during their earliest years, their bodies keep the score. This information is available to us if we learn how to see it and interpret its meaning.

The central element of character analysis is the idea that the mind and body are one. The traumas we experience and the defenses we create shape not only our minds, but also our brains and the musculoskeletal and motor activity of our bodies. While this perspective is more widely accepted today, it was a revolutionary concept a century ago, when mind and body were seen as distinct and separate from one another.

Psychological defenses, or character armor as Reich called them, were embodied in the bearing, posture, and attitudes of a client, which gave a great deal of additional information about a client's history over and above what was available to their conscious awareness and autobiographical memory. Reich believed that a client's behaviors and the quality of the therapeutic relationship were direct manifestations of how they defended themselves early in life against real and imagined dangers. Words can mislead both client and therapist, but the body doesn't know how to lie.

Our state of brain and mind is almost always manifest in our muscles (especially those in our faces), the direction of our gaze, the pace and depth of our breathing, the tone of our voice, the movements of our hands, and so on. Reich encouraged therapists to look beyond words and become careful observers of their client's entire being. For example, fear during childhood could trigger shallow breathing and shoulder tension in adulthood when a client is exposed to unconscious reminders of early stress. The client can honestly tell you they feel fine, yet you witness a parallel expression of their implicit memory systems through observed changes in their breathing and posture.

Another example could be that, as a result of insensitive or shaming parents, the child learns to protect themselves from all input from others and sends out an emissary, or false self, to engage in the world. This false self may be polite and compliant but doesn't trust anything other people say or do. As adults, they continue to live as the isolated child they needed to be to survive childhood. They can also convince themselves that their false self is their true self. We are learning now that these early experiences even alter brain development in ways that limit and distort the intake of sensory and social information in order to protect us from a hostile environment.

Because character armor is organized within systems of implicit and procedural memory, it is almost always invisible to its owner, even when their patterns of behavior are repeatedly pointed out to them. The client will not bring it up for discussion because it is not within the scope of their conscious awareness. It is, in a sense, an invisible prism through which the client sees the world, interprets its meanings, and navigates life. They are unable to see its negative impact on their relationships and work, and attribute the problems they experience to external causes. Their belief in the external causes of their difficulties is often unshakable. Enough evidence has to be accumulated and presented in a manner that allows them to consider that their behavior may be contributing to the problem. Someone with strong narcissistic defenses will hold them tightly because they are too vulnerable to tolerate the experience of their imperfections.

A therapist who believes that the surface content is all there is tends to overestimate the importance of what is said, leading to what Reich (1945) called "a catastrophic comprehension of the psychic surface." Catastrophic in the sense that the client and therapist believe that therapy is taking place while the character armor remains intact and the symptoms unresolved. It is this overvaluing of articulating content, digging up core beliefs, recounting traumatic memories, analyzing dreams, and so on, while ignoring the way the client interacts with the therapist, that leads to stagnation in therapy. While the client might be cooperative and even complimentary to the therapist, these may be bricks in a wall concealing distrust, skepticism, or a condescending or derogatory attitude toward the therapist and the therapy itself; "This may help others, but it can't help me."

THE THERAPIST'S CHALLENGE

What interests me in life is curiosity, challenge, the
good fight with its victories and defeats.
PAULO COELHO

The fact that character armor is invisible to the client means that it is the therapist's job to help the client become conscious of it and its relationship to the problems for which the client seeks help. This process creates a great challenge to the therapist. In our everyday relationships, we operate under an implicit social agreement: "I won't call you on your act if you don't call me on mine." True therapy violates this agreement and puts the therapist at risk for having to deal with a client's negative transference. This is especially hard for therapists who, because of their own character armor, are either avoidant or terrified of anger, conflict, or confrontation.

Exploring negative transference requires an intense here-and-now focus, as opposed to discussion about safe topics outside of therapeutic interactions. In order to make progress, character armor first has to be made conscious and seen for what it is, a defense against anxiety, pain, and loss. Second, it has to be made ego dystonic, which means that the client comes to see and experience it as incongruent with the person they are or want to become. Character armor needs to come to be seen as a set of symptoms, apart from the self, so it can become the focus of treatment. In Reich's words, the patient has to come to realize first that he is resisting, then how the resistance is expressed, and finally against what. Once this separation is attained, a client can root it out, understand its impact, and engage in experiments to learn and practice change.

The job of the therapist in rendering the armor visible—making the king realize that he has no clothes—is a difficult one. To the degree to which you are successful, your client will have strong emotional reactions that will often be targeted at you. Making a defense conscious can also have the effect of weakening its ability to protect us from emotion and, in some cases, renders it useless. The result is that the client's conscious awareness is no longer protected from the difficult emotions the armor was developed for in the first place. For example, if you are able to help someone see their grandiosity as a defense against feelings of shame, they may get in touch with with their primordial reaction to being abandoned early in life. Without the narcissistic defenses that have protected them, they are slung back into a painful past where they were vulnerable, alone, and terrified.

As an example, a client came complaining of how weak and "wimpy" his family and friends were and that they were blaming him for being mean and hostile. "What's wrong with the world?" he began. "When did everyone become such snowflakes?" The only reason he came to therapy was because his wife was threatening him with divorce and insisted he get help. The truth was, even when he claimed to be relaxed, he looked angry, tense, and ready to pounce. As I gently reflected this back to him over a number of months, he came to be aware of the tension he held in his body and what his "fighting stance" was. It was important that this defensive posture be validated in that it was developed to survive his violent mother and his dangerous neighborhood. His first reaction was to see everything as a fight, be quick to anger, and react defensively to most everything said to him.

This wasn't an easy process. There was considerable negative transference, leading him to say things like, "Don't tell me you're a snowflake too!" and "How do you survive being so sensitive?" I had to tolerate these attacks and stay on message. I repeatedly connected his attitude toward me to his early fight for survival and the fact that he no longer lived in that world. He struggled to come to grips with the fact that his present life didn't require fighting and, in fact, continuing his personal war was risking everything he had accomplished. As he put it, "Doc, you're trying to get me to embrace my inner snowflake." As he did, painful, violent memories would arise from his childhood, and he would regress back into his fighting stance. But he kept at it, and slowly experimented with being more relaxed and vulnerable with those around him to test whether he was truly safe. His mind knew it, but he still hadn't convinced his body. In his own way and on his own schedule, he slowly shifted to life during peacetime.

In stark contrast, character armor can also take the form of the good patient who superficially agrees with everything you say but refuses to bring anything from therapy into their everyday lives; the rigidly conventional client who organizes themselves by following rules; clients who cannot experience feelings and live compulsively driven lives; and those who secretly laugh at the therapist and everyone else. All of these represent common forms of adult character armor, originally formed as adaptations to early disruptions of attachment and attunement.

Most forms of character armor will include the client pushing forward content that will serve to keep the therapist occupied and away from key issues of their deeper narrative. The therapist's job is to see through these defenses and have a conceptualization of the origin and purpose of the defenses. Then we have to consistently steer the interaction toward the real issues and not take the bait of issues designed to distract us. This is why Reich says that resistance, especially about transference, cannot be taken up too soon, and that content interpretations about unconscious material cannot be held back long enough. This was a clear poke at his mentor Freud, but an important step forward in the development of psychotherapy.

It is important to remember here that character armor is organized at a time when the child is small and their brain immature. Parents, both good and bad, are experienced as gods, and highly emotional interactions are experienced as matters of life and death. Because immature brains process all information from an egocentric position, things that occur around a child—anger, fear, domestic violence, abandonment, death of a parent—are all experienced as their responsibility. Children blame themselves for all the pain that surrounds them—as Reich blamed himself for his mother's suicide—and character armor is built to manage these emotionally overwhelming experiences. The strength of the armor is usually proportional to the trauma that necessitated its construction.

While character armor is initially created by the client to protect them from pain and anxiety from without, it later becomes a rigid shell limiting their engagement in life. This is why Reich believed that we tend to remain sick and repetitively engage in unhealthy and self-destructive behavior. In opposition to Freud, who believed that we continue to engage in irrational behaviors in an unconscious effort to heal, Reich thought that we respond to the world through the prism of our early defenses. This results in the patterns that keep us circling through self-defeating patterns of behavior. Put in a slightly different way, character armor creates strategies for dealing with the child's world, yet repeatedly fails in adult settings and relationships.

Given that we interpret these invisible strategies as reason, we continue to employ them only to fail again and again. In other words, we operate with a logic that worked in the context of our early childhood, but is no longer a good match for our current adult situation. When therapists don't understand this underlying process, they miss the complex adaptation to early stress and blame the client for not wanting to get well. These ideas protect the therapist's ego and help them avoid taking responsibility for therapeutic failures.

Reich would say that character armor calls into question both the Freudian and Rogerian concepts that the direction of therapy should be left to the client. To the degree that Reich is correct, this could result in extended periods of misdirection. Both Freud and Rogers had legitimate counterarguments to Reich's position, and it falls on us to choose the approach and strategies we use.

NEGATIVE TRANSFERENCE

If one is not to get into a rage sometimes,
what is the good of being friends?
GEORGE ELIOT

According to Reich, one of the key reasons that therapy stalls is that the therapist fails to recognize, name, and process negative transference. It makes sense that negative transference lies near the core of defenses because the armor itself is born of the fears and failures of attunement from early in life. The reactions to these failures become the core of attachment insecurities and anger at those we needed to be there for us. Expressions of negative transference range from screaming, hitting, and breaking things in your office to subtle microaggressions that are easy to miss if you aren't looking for them. I've had clients who very gently criticize my clothing, offer to raise their payments because I don't seem to be doing well, or tell me that one of my interpretations is "cute." All of these interactions could be shrugged off, missed, or normalized; worse, I could tap into my own shame and make therapy about defending my own ego.

A client's defenses against others become manifest in the transference and keep them, as one of my clients described it, "behind a wall." It is from behind this wall that the client manages their identity in the therapy as they had to manage it early in life with key attachment figures. Thus, the content in therapy can be a defensive maneuver expressed by the personality (avatar) they send into relationships, while the client stays safely behind a wall. It is in these situations that a focus on the transference, character armor, and a here-and-now approach is essential to progress.

The difficulty of this work and the danger experienced by the client necessitates a strong motivation to heal and a well-developed therapeutic alliance. The part of the client that is dedicated to healing needs to be well aligned with the therapist so they can together get to know the frightened child within. When clients behave in seemingly incoherent, illogical, or self-defeating ways, we work to enlist their curiosity about what part of them is engaged in defensive maneuvers. For a client to get to the point where they can say, "I want you to know that I feel angry at you and want to walk out of your office," instead of doing it, shows that they have become curious about the transference experience. They have learned that these emotions (when not a reaction to actual errors by the therapist) are part of their implicit memory systems and likely to be defensive. "You're a bad therapist" slowly evolves to "I wonder why I'm so pissed off at you," which evolves to "I'm pissed off at my father." This reflects the shift from acting out to acting in.

GETTING TO THE FEELINGS

An advantage of the emotions is that they lead us astray.
OSCAR WILDE

Most therapists have at least a vague sense that emotions are important and love to ask, "How does that make you feel?"—a totally reasonable question that sometimes gets you where you want to go. All too often, however, a therapist will continue to ask the question and get frustrated with seemingly evasive answers. The dissociation of emotions and bodily states from conscious awareness may be an aspect of their invisible defenses and character armor. Intellectualized clients may respond with thoughts instead of feelings; clients who were parentified during childhood may respond with how they think others think they should feel; still others will look within to find their feelings, and find nothing there.

I began my work with the naive assumption that everyone was capable of being aware of what they are feeling. I also assumed that it was only through repression, denial, or resistance that they wouldn't be forthcoming about what was going on inside them. Experience combined with an understanding of how emotions are processed within the brain has led me to change my thinking. **I now believe that some of our clients are truly unaware of their bodily states and feelings.**

Repeatedly asking clients how they feel only makes them feel frustrated, ashamed, angry. Many clients with avoidant and disorganized attachment schemas or chronic high levels of arousal may have no idea how to answer these questions. Some clients even make up emotions just to get us to stop harassing them. Being able to recognize and articulate how you are feeling is an ability learned during childhood when mirrored by attuned others, and helped to find words that match their subjective states.

If you accept the possibility that not everyone knows what they feel about any particular topic, the next step is to develop a theory of why this is so. If there is a neurodevelopmental or neurological deficit or a disconnection syndrome (e.g., autism or alexithymia), this may not be a fruitful avenue for psychotherapy. If it seems, however, that the client's inability to detect or express their feelings is the result of an early mirroring deficit, then this may be a very important focus of therapy. This is an area where psychotherapy closely parallels the parenting process and employs strategies similar to active attunement and mirroring.

Think about sitting across from your one-year-old who has just finished a scoop of ice cream. As they look into the empty bowl, their facial expression gradually shifts from pleasure to distress. You can easily guess that they want more ice cream and experience the empty bowl as distressing. As their face turns from a pout to tears, your own expression might change from pleasure to sadness, mirroring theirs. You might say something like, "Oh honey, your ice cream is gone and you want more! Does that make you feel sad?" Now you might watch your baby's face turn from sadness to anger as they bang their spoon on the table and flip their bowl onto the floor. You might say, "Oh my, you were sad that there was no ice cream, and now you seem mad!" Of course, these are guesses about the child's internal state, but I suspect that they are pretty good guesses.

The processes of emotional attunement, matching the child's facial expressions, and putting words to what the child is feeling are all aspects of the mirroring process. It is from countless interactions like these that a child learns that (1) their bodily states are tied to their emotions; (2) their emotions are seen by others; and (3) that there are words that describe these feelings that can be shared with others. Children who grow up without adequate mirroring can remain in the dark about all three of these things their entire lives. For these clients, the mirroring they receive in therapy may be their first experience of realizing they are being seen. It can't be assumed that they can answer or even understand the question, "How does that make you feel?" Spending a lifetime with dissociated emotions leads to the formation of a variety of defenses, makes self-soothing more difficult, and can lead to the experience of being an anthropologist from Mars.

Instead of asking these clients how they feel, get in touch with your emotions and consider how you might have felt if you were in their shoes. In other words, start where you think your client might need to go, and go there yourself. Shuttle down into your body and feel what it feels like, get a sense of the words that describe it, and how you might feel if you had to share this for the first time (as a child might). Create a state of mind and body that is as close as you can make it to where you hypothesize your client's emotions are. Ask them to be aware of their breathing and become as centered as they can. It is from this place that you can ask them to tell you about the experiences you believe were painful for them. They will most likely try and divert their attention (and yours) from the emotions associated with these memories, but stay anchored in your feelings, accept whatever process they need to engage in, and never assume that you are on the right track. Everything is information—use constant reassessment and remain as flexible and open as possible.

Some clients may need you to start things off through disclosure. I might share a story of my own with emotions similar to those feelings I believe they might be having. Sometimes I will share how I imagine I might feel if I had been in their situation, the whole time keeping in mind that these are hypotheses and should be presented as possibilities and not edicts from on high. Play with these ideas loosely and let your clients accept, modify, or reject them. If you are on the right track, you will find your way to where you need to be. The important issues never go away; they just go into temporary hiding. Remember that during childhood, it takes countless iterations of the same conversations with our children for them to clearly express what they are feeling. We need to be patient with our clients, especially if they have been surviving for decades without information from their inner worlds. This means they are used to assessing situations based on ideas and strategies—and questions like "How do you feel?" may be a foreign language.

CHAPTER 9

WHAT DO ZOMBIES DO FOR FUN?

Symbolism is no mere idle fancy or corrupt degeneration;
it is inherent in the very texture of human life.
ALFRED NORTH WHITEHEAD

At this point I thought it would be interesting to share a case with you as well as my reflections along the way. I'll bracket these thoughts, so that you can easily distinguish them from my interactions during the session. Keep in mind that there are hundreds of decision points during every session, and following any one of them can prove fruitful, or not. The way I do therapy is but one of many, so as you read along, be thinking about what you might do if confronted with similar situations. Pay attention to your own associations and ideas, and how you might choose to interact with my client.

DANIELLE

On the advice of an old friend, Danielle called to make an appointment for an initial meeting to see if we might be a good fit. While it is not uncommon for potential clients to say they are looking for a therapist who feels like a good fit, it seemed to have a special significance for Danielle. She told me she needed to take me for "a road test" before she decided to buy, which made us both laugh. Danielle, like many clients, told me she was struggling with stress, anxiety, and depression. Her tone of voice and her emphasis on each syllable caught my attention. The mechanistic quality of her voice and her choice of words made me wonder whether this was a distancing defense.

Danielle appeared in my waiting room later that week dressed in a perfectly tailored business suit. A strikingly beautiful African American woman, she shook my hand with a smile, and said, "I'm here for my road test. I hope your tank is full!" She was engaging, intelligent, and articulate, and I liked her immediately; at the same time, her tension and bodily rigidity were palpable, in line with the stress and anxiety she described during our call. I imagined her walking a tightrope high above the ground, self-conscious of her every movement. Later, as I learned about her childhood, I suspected that her persona had been well crafted to protect against threat. An occasional pained facial expression and regularly shifting postures seemed to reflect her fear and apprehension.

At first, Danielle briefly alluded to the challenges of her childhood but jumped to talking about high school. "I threw myself into my classes and sports 110%." She seemed to carry this "110%" strategy into her work as a systems analyst for Google, where she experienced a rapid rise through the ranks. "I was a straight-A student and now I'm a straight-A employee . . . and it never hurts being a Black woman surrounded by nervous white men," she added with well-coordinated wags of her head and right index finger. "They let you rise just a bit so they can show you off at board meetings and put your picture in the annual report; being good at your job is an unexpected bonus." All the while she seemed to be carefully watching my reaction. Perhaps her reference to nervous white men was a test. I reflected that she probably gave them quite a big bonus, to which she replied, "You're damn straight!" with a wry smile.

I noticed that when Danielle said, "I threw myself into school," she said it similarly to the way she said, "a good fit" when referring to her search for a therapist. Did these two things share some special relationship or symbolic meaning, or were they just ways she emphasized certain words? I also wondered if her comment about nervous white men, a group of which I happen to be a member, was a message to me. Was I being evaluated for my ability to stay with her through difficult times or my ability to risk her ire by being truthful? As a successful Black woman, I assumed she had plenty of experience managing her identity across all sorts of situations. I certainly wanted to create an environment within which she could feel safe to say whatever came to mind.

While we shouldn't make too much of these very early interactions, it's difficult to keep our minds from automatically generating ideas, categories, and connections. I've always found it best to keep my early impressions to myself, make a note of them, and bring them up to the client later if I gather more information to support them. It's important not to share too many associations early on. You don't want to turn the relationship into a guessing game that is way ahead of where your client is. It also runs the risk of turning your client into a passive observer.

During our second session, I asked Danielle why she had decided to come to therapy now. "I've always known, at some level, that I've been depressed and fight it off by staying busy," she said. "I keep taking on more responsibilities at work, and my to-do lists are longer than one person could ever keep up with." "This sounds like a part of your '110%' life strategy," I replied, "but what made you come for help now?" At this point I noticed her eyes welling up with tears. She started fanning her face with her hands, grabbed a couple of tissues, and began to carefully wipe her tears. "This is what's been happening lately. I just start crying for no reason. I must be going crazy." She sat in silence, her body stiff, upright, as she seemed to try to pull her tears back up into her eyes, apologizing for her emotions. It was clear how embarrassed and frightened she was by her vulnerability.

As she strained to compose herself, she looked off to the side as if watching a scene play out before her eyes. After a while, she hesitantly began to speak. "I was in my backyard yesterday when I noticed that I had forgotten to take my favorite plant inside after watering it last week. When I saw the burnt dead thing, and realized what had happened, I sat down, put my head into my hands, and cried. I thought I must be having a nervous breakdown. I was sad about the plant, but I knew I was really feeling sorry for myself. I felt like the neglected one, forgotten, drying up, dead inside. I was dying because nobody cares for me, not even me. I won't let anyone close enough to even try. Look at me—I was raised to believe that the worst thing I could do was feel sorry for myself, and that's exactly what I'm doing." She returned to carefully drying her tears.

> I reflected back on her looking for the "right fit" and wondered if she meant someone who could see her, attune to her emotions, and tolerate being with them. Someone who could see past the hypercompetent adult to the exhausted, neglected, and frightened child. Perhaps Danielle's early lessons not to feel sorry for herself might have come to mean she should never feel anything negative. She may have grown up believing, as

many people do, that emotions are weaknesses that put you in danger. Perhaps this was even true in her family. I imagined that Danielle needed someone who could stand with her and her emotions, so she could learn to stop running away from the feelings that overwhelmed her as a child. This was far deeper than the race and gender politics she had to play each day; it was about a child's need to be loved.

Danielle continued to cry as I sat with her in silence, collapsed into the position she had taken on her garden bench. After a while, I asked her if she ever had someone she could share her feelings with. She didn't answer my question directly, but began to share some of the details of her childhood. She told me how her father had abandoned the family when she was 10, and how her mother worked two jobs to support Danielle and her three siblings. Because her mother was gone most of the time and Danielle was the oldest, many chores and child care responsibilities fell on her small shoulders. When her mother was around, she was usually too tired to talk and would stiffen and push Danielle away when she tried to be affectionate. Danielle said, "It always felt like she was disappointed in me, no matter how much I did for her and the family. Maybe she was too beaten down to feel anything."

"I worked hard at school and hard at home," she continued. "It felt like my only chance to make it. What was even worse was that I knew my mother hated her life, and I assumed it was my fault. If I wasn't around, she could have worked less, gone out on dates, and had fun. Without me and the kids, she could have had the life she needed and deserved. Every so often, when one of us would make a mess or get in trouble at school, she would call out, 'Why did I ever have children?' When I was really young, I thought she had a direct connection with God, and I imagined him sitting up in heaven, nodding his head in agreement. The worst was when I would hear her crying at night and praying to God to take her to him; that would really frighten me. What would we do if she passed? We'd end up on the streets begging for food from strangers, or even worse, separated by the social work ladies.

"I knew I had to be as little of a problem as I could and do whatever I could to make my mother's life easier. I cleaned the house, washed the dishes, and never asked for anything or complained when I was sick. I figured that anything I needed from her might push her over the edge and God might take her. Whenever I would make a mistake or cause her extra bother, she would start talking to Jesus about how she was suffering, and I would panic and have a hard time breathing."

It seemed that Danielle felt comfortable enough to stay with these difficult feelings. I thought that a key component of being the right fit might be silence, active listening, and not trying to minimize or, worse, invalidate her feelings in any way. My silence and attention may have been a tacit communication that she wasn't with someone like her friends who needed her to cheer up. I had to be observant of whether my more passive stance would be experienced by her as meaning that I was too nervous to say anything, so I made sure to make periodic comments to show her I was all in with her.

In order to understand Danielle's experience, it is important to realize how she would have understood her mother's lamentations at such a young age. Children often think their parents have a direct line to god, and many parents support this fantasy to keep their children in line. Many still believe that prayers go directly to a man sitting on a cloud. For children, abandonment equals death, and if your father can abandon you (which he did), so can your mother, and so can God.

Danielle continued, "My mother needed what I needed, someone who could take care of her and make her feel safe, just like my grandmother, and who knows how many generations before her. She did have God, but the Jesus thing never worked for me. It seemed like making up an imaginary friend, and imaginary didn't cut it for me. I need a real person who's the right fit for me.

I imagined my father living in a nice house, taking care of his new kids, and giving them all the things I needed. I daydreamed about him showing up out of the blue, getting back together with my mom, and taking care of all of us. I would close my eyes and think about him picking me up, holding me in his strong arms, and telling me that everything was going to be just fine. But if I allowed myself to think about him too long, I just wanted to beat his face in. Then I'd feel guilty about being angry and want to melt into his arms. Bouncing back and forth between these feelings tore me apart."

I felt so sad hearing this story and had a fantasy that I could go back in time and rescue her. My countertransference was in full gear, and I was having memories of my father abandoning my family when I was young. These experiences had shaped Danielle's self-image, as they had mine, making her feel unlovable and unworthy of the attention of others. I found that she had few friends, staying at work late instead of going out, and still visiting her mother and taking care of her in any way she could. She seemed to feel truly alone, even when surrounded by others.

I began to think of her entertaining personality as one of the ways she took care of others, the way she began our relationship to protect me from her feelings. As the weeks passed, I could see her slowly letting down this defense and focusing more on herself and her inner world. Although we never discussed it openly, she still seemed to carry the hope that we were a good fit. I continued to keep my input to a minimum at this early stage. I felt that she was not only teaching me valuable information about her life, but also getting practice in feeling and expressing her emotions in the presence of another. She still likely had more layers of defense, but it was certainly a step closer to her true self. I had to show her that I accepted and cared for her even when she wasn't being smart and witty.

During our fourth session, I asked her what her relationships were like. "I grew up in Baltimore," she replied, "and when I went to college in Michigan, I didn't stay connected with any of my childhood friends. Most of them dropped out of high school and had babies. I made a few friends during college but left them behind when I came to LA to take the Google job. Since I got here about two years ago, I haven't made any good friends. My work colleagues are like children, and spend most of their time on Instagram and playing video games. Lots of giggling white girls I can't relate to. They don't seem motivated to accomplish much and spend a lot of time killing time. It's as if their intelligence and motivation have been sucked into their phones."

As she described her current life, Danielle became increasingly deflated. I wondered whether her feelings of disconnection from others triggered memories and emotions of isolation during her childhood. "I've tried to get to know some of the girls at work, but they seem like shadows, speak in clichés, and don't share their real feelings about anything. It's like all they can do is copy what they hear other people saying." Danielle sank into her feelings of aloneness, and I followed her. Loneliness seemed to be a core issue for her, one that we would have to fully explore. "I don't belong in my life now, and I don't belong where I came from. I'm a refugee."

At this point I began to wonder if Danielle's early experiences of abandonment and seeing herself as the cause of her mother's suffering had formed a sense of self around feelings of worthlessness and shame. Perhaps the reason she kept her distance from others and focused on their shortcomings was to stay safe from being rejected once again, from the experience of being pushed away when she sought affection. It would be important for her to eventually risk being vulnerable with a carefully chosen potential friend who would be a good fit for her.

During the following session, perhaps as a way to give us both a break from the dark feelings we had been discussing, I asked her if there was something she really enjoyed doing. At first, she had a hard time coming up with something, but after a while her eyes brightened, and a smile appeared that I hadn't seen since our first sessions. She looked at me with a devilish smile and said, "Zombies." I gave her a confused look—a signal for her to elaborate. "You know, zombie movies like *Invasion of the Body Snatchers* and *I Am Legend*. Not being a fan myself, I asked her to teach me about zombies, and she did, in great detail. I learned that there are zombies from other planets, from below ground, and those who become zombies because they had unknowingly been intimate with a zombie. Sometimes it is clear that the folks staggering toward you, body parts in disarray, are zombies. Other times, they are harder to spot because they look and act just like us.

While I can't say I found zombies interesting, I was captivated by Danielle's enthusiasm and knowledge of the topic. She seemed to turn into a much younger, less oppressed, and more spontaneous person. I could see that the topic had shifted her into a state of mind where she was not feeling her sadness or loneliness. But why zombies? Why did she feel so connected to such repulsive creatures? "What's it like to be a zombie?" I asked. "What do they think about? What do they do for fun?" By her expression, it was clear that I had asked a stupid question. "Zombies don't think or feel anything, silly goose—they just are." I smiled when I heard her call me a silly goose, a phrase I hadn't heard for a very long time that reminded me of my grandparents.

My smile immediately froze her. It seemed to have triggered a shutdown (shame) response. When she asked why I had smiled, I told her, and she was very apologetic. "I'm sorry if I insulted you. I shouldn't have called my doctor a silly goose." (She had let herself slip for a moment and hadn't filtered this remark.) I told her that I truly wasn't offended, but that I was curious if anyone had ever called her a silly goose, maybe as a child. "That's what my mother called me when I told her I was worried or upset about something!" "To worry meant that you were silly?" I asked. "Yes," she replied, "and also to be angry, upset, depressed, or confused. We didn't have the privilege of such nonsense. The only smart things to do were to be happy and busy—everything else was a problem. If I complained about anything, my mother would tell me to do something to make myself feel better. Take a shower, have some ice cream, clean the refrigerator, stay busy, and don't think bad thoughts."

"It sounds as if you took that lesson to heart," I offered, raising my voice at the end to make it more of a question than a statement. Danielle sat quietly and eventually said, "I learned my lesson well," then lapsed into another silence. After a while, I asked her if she realized she was quiet and whether she might like to share her thoughts. She said, "At first, when you said I 'took that lesson to heart,' I felt confused and tried to focus, but my mind kept going blank. Then I tried to remember what we were talking about before I called you a silly goose, and remembered that you asked what zombies do for fun."

> I was so impressed by her intelligence, her strength, and her honesty. How could her father have been so stupid as to abandon someone like this? Now I wanted to kick the shit out of him as well. Countertransference. Ya think?

She said, "When I was quiet, I was first trying to think of more things to tell you about zombies, but instead, I started to wonder if I'm a zombie. I stagger through space, going from thing to thing, but have no experience of being alive. Then I thought about my mother saying, 'Don't stop, don't feel, don't look back, keep moving forward.' I started to think that maybe if you can't feel most of your feelings, you are kind of a zombie. I guess there is another way you can become a zombie—you can be raised by one and taught to be one. Keep staggering forward and get things done. Then I heard you ask me if I realized I was being silent. I hadn't, but then I did."

After another long silence, Danielle asked me in a child-like voice, "Is there a way to stop being a zombie?" It was my turn to be silent as I considered potential responses to her question. After a while, I said, "My best guess is that you've already started. You've begun to see how you've avoided feelings, and are beginning to have them and share them with me. From now on, it will be your choice, moment to moment, to make the decision to move toward or away from your feelings, your humanness. Now we can start to imagine how things might have been different for you if your mother could acknowledge and help you to understand your feelings. We can't go back in time, but we can start this process now. If you can become aware of when you are cutting off your feelings, or hear a voice in your head saying, 'Don't be a silly goose,' you can say, 'Thank you, Mom, for trying to protect me from the pain you've suffered, but I'm strong enough to experience my emotions. The need to be a zombie has passed.'" Danielle hugged herself as she wept softly.

> What we find appealing, especially if it is in stark contrast to our everyday persona, may well have a deep symbolic value. Loving to watch zombies stagger through life is a meaningful entertainment choice in the context of the deeper narrative of Danielle's life. This may, at first, have seemed like a superficial or avoidant choice on her part, but by focusing on zombies, Danielle quickly brought us both to a key (and perhaps central) issue of her life.

I was extremely impressed with Danielle's openness and honesty, with both me and herself. The speed with which she made the connection between her dead plant, her fascination with zombies, and her lack of emotional connection to life was remarkable. That being said, habits of a lifetime are not easily broken. To understand something does not mean you have been delivered from it; it merely means that you have a way to use your mind to begin the long process of changing your brain.

Another challenge Danielle would face was her loyalty to her mother's suffering. Danielle is capable of being happy and achieving things never available to her mother. If she gets better, Danielle will be emotionally abandoning her mother to be alone in her pain. Her challenge will be to come to peace with this separation and the betrayal of their implicit agreement to be in pain together and keep staggering forward at all costs.

Being raised to deny your emotions and live through the eyes of others shapes thousands of neural circuits which can shape our experiences for a lifetime. This wiring can then result in the suppression or inhibition of an awareness of emotion, our ability to perceive our external worlds, and engage in behaviors we need later in life. This results in an experience of self, social relationships, and identity that have to be rewired, connection by connection, over time. It doesn't mean that someone has to be in therapy forever, but it does require developing the tools for identifying old reflexes and making new decisions about our thoughts, feelings, and behaviors. Danielle has to extend the dialogue she shared with me to an ongoing internal dialogue with herself as she moves through her day, paying attention to inadvertently slipping into zombie mode, redirecting her attention to what is happening somatically and emotionally within her, and then including this previously ignored information into her moment-to-moment conscious experience.

THE PROCESS OF CHANGE

Only the wisest and stupidest of men never change.
CONFUCIUS

It is helpful to caution clients both at the beginning of therapy and many times along the way that the reflexes and habits formed in childhood are deeply entrenched and difficult to change. The metric of progress can't be the disappearance of long-standing habits through a flash of insight. If this is what clients expect, they will become discouraged and give up. In my estimation, the best metrics of success are the slow and subtle changes in the intensity and latency of symptoms over time. In other words, how strong are the old impulses, and how long does it take for us to become aware of and interrupt them? In Danielle's case, one question would be, how strongly are you trapped in your zombie self? The second is, how long were you in your zombie self before you realized it and remembered to go back to being human?

As Danielle worked in therapy to understand and change this part of herself, she built more and more conscious awareness and cortical circuitry dedicated to remembering to observe herself. As these neural circuits grow, they exert more descending modulation on the bottom-up impulses and old reflexes organized in childhood. As these circuits build in strength, the intensity of the regression to old ways of behavior will decrease and the time (latency) between being triggered and conscious awareness that she has been triggered will decrease.

The metrics of intensity and latency allow us to see stages of progress as opposed to being discouraged because we have not been able to completely inhibit patterns of a lifetime from one session to the next. Danielle and many other clients will say things like, "I realized the next day what I was doing and was able to remember what we talked about and how to take control of the situation." As the months went by, she was able to say that she was in a zombie state for a few hours and then a few minutes. Finally, she was able to be aware of the triggers that made her regress as it was happening and decide not to go there. Clients will say, "Six months ago, this would have sent me into a tailspin that would have lasted weeks. This time I was upset for a few hours, got over it, and got back on track." The work to decrease latency and intensity reflects the rebalancing of cortical and subcortical neurodynamics, giving the cortex modulatory and inhibitory control over habitual and dysfunctional thoughts, feelings, and behaviors. Now that's true and measurable progress.

CHAPTER 10

FROM TERROR TO SAFETY

There is no safety in numbers, or in anything else.
JAMES THURBER

Experiencing pain comes with being human. All too often, the type of everyday pain we all experience is overshadowed by something that causes us terror and threatens our physical and emotional survival. For some of us, this terror becomes traumatic, and some develop post-traumatic stress disorder (PTSD). There is a wide range of reactions to traumatic experiences and ways that PTSD manifests in its victims. Some of us become indignant, angry, even violent gladiators on a mission to avenge the wrongs we have endured. These individuals are often able to leverage their experiences into grit, resilience, and personal empowerment. When folks like these come to therapy, it is most often because they have burned themselves out fighting the good fight while neglecting rest, self-care, and restoration.

FROM VICTIMIZATION, TO ASSERTION, TO SAFETY

I am interested in power that is moral,
that is right and that is good.
MARTIN LUTHER KING JR.

Through the years, I have been particularly impressed with how difficult it has been to help my clients navigate a direct therapeutic path from the frozen state of trauma (victimization, prey animal, beta, or omega status) to a place of peace and safety. They read endless self-help books, practice meditation and yoga, or listen to music, to help calm them in the moment. Unfortunately, these practices do not touch the core of the physiological dysregulation at the heart of PTSD. In contrast, when I have been successful, it is when I've used an indirect path via assertiveness, anger, and personal empowerment. Taking cues from those who react to victimization by becoming gladiators, there is something about anger and assertiveness that seems essential to the process of healing trauma in this group of clients. My suspicion is that the explanation exists in the way our nervous system is organized and functions. You will see a reaction like this in my client Jay, whom I will share with you in the pages to come.

Anger and assertiveness evolved along with nurturing behavior as part of child-rearing, attachment, and pair bonding. After all, we not only need to hold and feed our children, we also have to protect them from harm. Many a mild-mannered person has been known to turn into a tiger when they see their children in danger. When we are not nurtured as children, we can learn not to nurture ourselves, even though we may retain the ability to take care of and protect others. This leads us to feel like mice in a world full of cats—everything is frightening and potentially dangerous. Without the sense of safety that comes through being able to take care of ourselves, searching for peace though meditation, yoga, and loving kindness can't take away the core terror of being alive. **It seems as if we have to first reactivate our assertion, anger, and aggression, in other words, be able to protect ourselves when necessary, before we can find peace.** Steve Porges (2011) has described what I think may be a parallel insight in his book, *The Polyvagal Theory*. Here is a brief explanation of his theory as I understand it.

Our nervous systems retain the evolutionary remnants of past survival strategies of fighting, fleeing, and freezing in response to threat. As you know, the sympathetic and para-sympathetic branches of the autonomic nervous system (ANS) control the processes of arousal and inhibition, respectively. The ANS works as the primitive on-off switch of our bodily arousal, but social relationships require finer regulation of arousal. For this purpose, and other functions of social engage-ment, the addition of the vagal arousal system created a sort of volume control. Thus, the ANS and vagal systems interact to regulate our arousal in response to both our physical and social environments.

The unmyelinated networks of the vagal system control bodily shutdown, immobilization, and freeze reactions in response to stress and danger, while the myelinated branch of the vagal system exerts a modulatory influence on sympa-thetic arousal. The vagal system is a complex feedback system that functions outside the spinal cord and provides us with another way of processing bodily and social information. This bottom-up information from the social engagement system, what Porges refers to as neuroception, also provides input for deeper interpersonal engagement such as reading facial expressions and knowing the meaning of an eye gaze.

The tone of the vagus refers to the system's ability to reg-ulate arousal. Children with poor vagal tone have difficulty suppressing emotions in situations demanding their attention, making it difficult for them to engage with their parents, sus-tain a shared focus with playmates, and maintain attention in the classroom. The development of vagal tone appears to be experience-dependent and impacted by the quality of attach-ment relationships during childhood. For example, infants with greater vagal tone elicit more attuned behavior from their parents that, in turn, helps them to develop greater emo-tional and physiological regulation. Good enough parenting not only teaches appropriate responses in challenging interpersonal situations, it also builds the neural circuitry required to successfully carry it out.

What does all this have to do with treating trauma? Here is the main idea: Trauma is capable of disrupting the homeostatic balance of these systems. A victim of trauma who gets locked into a dorsal vagal state can shut down and be unable to activate sympathetic or ventral vagal arousal. This leads them to feel helpless, cut themselves off from others, and disconnect from themselves. As social animals, separation from our troop renders us vulnerable to danger because for social animals, separation equals death. It also inhibits our ability to use our assertion, anger, and aggression to protect ourselves. The implication of this theory is that for those who become shut down and frozen with fear, you have to first activate the fight-flight response before you can rebalance arousal systems to attain an experience of safety.

Not surprisingly, the same physiology shapes the behaviors of predators and prey, as well as the interpersonal dynamics demonstrated in alpha, beta, and omega social status. If we are locked into the freeze reactions of a victim, we experience others as predators because we are unable to defend ourselves. The background emotion of our day-to-day experience is that of a vulnerable child, regardless of our size, age, or gender. What I would call channeling the gladiator, Porges would call activating the sympathetic nervous system and the smart vagus so you can safely engage with others. This becomes activated at any age when we confront our parents, get pulled over by the police, or meet people we experience as alphas.

How a client becomes activated depends on who they are and whether you can find the appropriate strategies to help bring out their inner warrior. Sometimes you can activate them by engaging them to fight for a cause or to help someone else. Assertiveness training and public speaking classes can be helpful, or martial arts, sports, role-playing, or whatever activates fear, provides skills to face it, and generates the courage to confront it. This can't be done intellectually or by proxy; it's a full-body experience that has to be engaged with in real-life circumstances.

MEMORIES EVERYWHERE

My yesterdays walk with me. They keep step, they are gray faces that peer over my shoulder.
WILLIAM GOLDING

Jay contacted me at his physician's request to make an appointment for therapy. He preferred not to speak over the phone and said he would "fill me in" when he saw me. Given that this was our initial visit, I reserved a two-hour slot for Jay so we wouldn't feel rushed. His physician and friend Carter called me later the same day to share his concerns. According to Carter, Jay had been "talking strange," and he had concerns that Jay might be either struggling with some memory disorder or considering suicide. Carter said, "He hasn't said anything specific about suicide or shown a preoccupation with death or dying—he just hasn't been himself."

Carter told me that Jay had retired a year ago at age 68 and went from being "very sharp and clear" to being "difficult to follow." We mused together that perhaps Jay was experiencing the beginnings of a dementing process, which may have led to his retirement. Carter told me that Jay was in good physical health as of his last checkup a few months ago and that Jay had asked him to call me to share his impressions before we met. Carter also wanted to let me know that he felt it was best if Jay communicate with him directly after our first visit. I assured Carter that I agreed with this strategy and would do my best to help his friend.

When I met Jay later that week, I was captured by his bright blue eyes, vitality, and excellent physical condition. He greeted me with an intense gaze and a firm handshake. I began by telling him I had spoken to Carter, which he already knew, and I asked him to fill me in. "Let me start by saying that I don't think there is anything wrong with my brain. Some things have been on my mind lately, and I may have made a mistake talking about them with Carter. He's a wonderful guy, and smart in his own way, but not a very deep thinker. He assumes if someone says something he doesn't understand, they must be getting Alzheimer's. Of course, he never considers that maybe he's the one who's demented." Jay laughed at his own joke, and I followed suit.

During our first session, I learned that Jay had grown up in a blue-collar neighborhood in St. Louis, just after World War II. His father ran a bar while his mother took care of the home, both of them "tough as nails, family-oriented, and proud of their Irish heritage." The family lived in a modest home, with Jay being the oldest of four boys. He described his parents as loving, strict, often volatile, and best kept at a distance when they had been drinking, which was a regular occurrence. Otherwise, the neighborhood was safe, with lots of kids to play with. "All of us were poor, but none of us knew it. Other than having to fight with bullies and avoid the priests, it was a great place to grow up." Jay felt that the mixture of safety and danger he grew up with prepared him for the real world. "Looking back, I learned hard work from my parents and the expectation that nothing is handed to you, and both have served me well."

After graduating from high school, Jay enlisted in the Marines and did a tour in Vietnam in 1967. During boot camp, the Marines seemed like a natural extension of Baltimore, but "Vietnam was another thing altogether. I had never known anyone who had died, let alone watching friends suffer and die in my arms. All I could do was to survive day to day, moment to moment, figuring that the next second, I could be dying in someone else's arms." Somehow, Jay had managed to survive a notorious ambush known as the Battle of July Two, when a quarter of his unit was killed. When he wasn't engaged in the fighting, he was carrying friends or unrecognizable pieces of Marines to the medic's foxhole. From then on, his unit was known as the Walking Dead.

HAUNTINGS

I have had dreams and I have had nightmares, but I have conquered my nightmares because of my dreams.
JONAS SALK

"For a long time after July Two," Jay told me, "I tried to avoid looking at anyone or even at myself in the mirror. If I did, I would see hands, arms, and legs disconnecting from the body, and guts flowing from their stomachs, all the things I saw in combat." He described how he would close his eyes and shake his head to get rid of the images that repeatedly haunted him. He had always considered himself a tough guy from the streets, but this was too much even for him. In Jay's words, it was "beyond the beyond." "Somewhere during that fight," he continued, "I lost my mind and never really got it back. I've been faking 'sane' ever since, holding it together for my family, friends, and myself.

"Over the years I've been offered therapy by the VA and told to go by some of my buddies, but I stuck to my guns and kept it all inside. I even found myself critical of the guys I met who broke and dropped out of society, and moved to the woods to try and keep the pain at bay. They knew they were walking time bombs and wanted to get away from people before they accidentally killed someone. My therapy has been keeping busy and staying as distracted as possible. I've always played and worked hard, and never allowed a quiet moment. For some reason, it doesn't seem to be working anymore, and it feels like what happened in Vietnam has finally caught up with me. I guess I always thought it would."

I asked him to describe what it meant to lose his mind. He fell into a silence. Eventually he continued, "It's hard for me to put into a few words, but I can tell you what I experienced." Then another long silence. "I've never talked to anyone about this before. Get the straitjacket ready." I could sense how difficult it was for Jay, so I took the opportunity to tell him that I had been working with combat veterans for decades and had heard a lot about what it was like.

I told him to take his time and do his best. After a minute or two of silence, Jay began to speak. "There were times when I was gone from the battlefield. I mean I was physically there, but my mind was gone. In the middle of a firefight, I'd be playing stickball with my brothers on the street in front of our house. Then I'd be back again. Sometimes, if we were pinned down by shelling or snipers, I'd start laughing, thinking I was home watching the Three Stooges on TV. It didn't feel like imagination. It felt real, and sometimes it was impossible to keep myself where I was. This was really frightening—what if we get overrun and I'm laughing at the Three Stooges? We all depended on each other. We had to have each other's backs. What if someone else got killed because I couldn't stay in my body? I still don't know how many guys we lost because I was busy being crazy.

"I bet you're wondering what this old news has to do with what's going on with me now. The strange thing is that it's happening again. I'm starting to come loose in time again, and float off into memories and fantasy. Sometimes I find myself back in Con Thien—that's where our forward base was in Vietnam—talking to some of the guys that died on July

Two. I know they're dead but they don't, like that movie with the kid that sees the dead people. Sometimes I'm back in St. Louis, listening to my parents talking on the back porch on a summer night. I can hear ice tinkling in their glasses and the music coming from cars as they drive by the house, the Four Tops singing 'Baby I Need Your Loving.' One of my favorites is being back with Charlotte, my first daughter, soon after she was born. I would spend hours rocking her, kissing her angel hair, smelling her head as she slept on my chest." Jay snapped out of his reverie, looked at me with wide eyes, and asked, "What's happening to me?"

After a pause, I took a breath and said, "You've been through a lot, Jay, but you obviously aren't crazy." I assured him that I had worked with many people who had lost their minds, but that he wasn't one of them. "At the very least," I continued, "the emergence of all of these memories and what seems to be their spontaneous appearance must be pretty confusing." "It is very confusing," Jay said, "and when I told Carter, he seemed to think I was having a nervous breakdown or getting demented." "Don't worry," I told Jay. "Whatever it is, we'll get to the bottom of it, but let me ask you—when did you first start having these memories come back to you? I mean recently, not when you were in Vietnam."

After reflecting a while, Jay said, "The first time was about a year ago when I was making preparations to retire. I started imagining what I was going to do with my time. That's when I began having memories about my kids, the war, my childhood—and the more I remembered, the more I remembered. By the time I actually retired, it seemed like I spent most of my time dreaming. Maybe imagining things isn't good for me—better to keep focused on what I'm doing. Maybe retiring was a mistake." It was getting close to the end of our first hour, so I suggested we take a 10-minute break. Jay seemed grateful to have the chance to relax and get a cup of coffee.

FIRST THOUGHTS

It is a very mixed blessing to be brought back from the dead.
KURT VONNEGUT

While Jay was on break, I sat, took a few notes, and reflected on the last hour. My best guess at this point was that he was neither going crazy" nor experiencing dementia. In my experience, clients who are experiencing a psychotic break seldom reflect on it, because it is both overwhelming and completely self-evident to them that what they are experiencing is true. The confusion, disorientation, and overwhelming fear usually make it impossible for them to think about it objectively.

It was altogether possible that Jay was at the beginning of a dementing process, accelerated by his retirement and the changes of routine that come with it. When people are beginning to lose neurons in their frontal and temporal lobes, as often occurs in dementia, they can be propped up for a considerable time by the familiar routines of past decades. It's when they change schedule or location, or lose a spouse that the deficits begin to reveal themselves more dramatically. If the evidence for dementia mounted, I would refer him to a neurologist for an evaluation. I wanted to find out if he retired by choice or was forced to retire due to diminishing capabilities. Consultation with family members and friends is also a good source of information.

Another possibility was that he was suffering symptoms of untreated and unresolved PTSD from his combat experiences that might be emerging now due to the loss of the structure and distraction of his work. As he described his life of hard work and hard play, I wondered if the time and opportunity to look inside had opened him up to a flood of disturbing thoughts, feelings, and memories that he had suppressed for many decades. What Jay described as becoming "loose in time" sounded like an adaptive dissociative defense against the overwhelming and inescapable fear he felt during his combat experiences. These types of reactions are not at all uncommon for those overwhelmed by terror. It sounds like even contemplating retirement sent his brain into a panic to direct him to maintain his work to distract him from his inner world.

You may have noticed how confidently I said, "We'll get to the bottom of it." This was neither an expression of certainty nor grandiose confidence, but a strategic decision based on how anxious Jay was about what was happening to him. The placebo effect is very powerful and can be tied to a doctor's communication of certainty—a potent tool for healing. Of course, there are no guarantees in psychotherapy, but the client's belief that they have a competent, loyal, and steadfast partner in the healing process is essential. That Jay has survived, with all the success he has experienced in his life (despite carrying this emotional burden), bodes well for both successful treatment and a good recovery. If it turns out that he is also suffering the beginning of a dementing process, we will work together to navigate that challenge as well.

MOVING AHEAD

> Trauma has the power to destroy and the
> power to transform and resurrect.
> PETER A. LEVINE

"So, we have a general time frame and a context when these experiences began—that's a good start. Tell me, Jay," I continued, "did you ever speak to anyone about July Two or your time in combat?" "You mean a therapist?" Jay asked. I responded, "A therapist, or your buddies, family, anyone?" He said, "Not really. I'm not into all that band of brothers stuff, and nobody else wants to hear about severed arms and spilled guts."

"Have you thought about it much over the last 50 years?" I asked. "Not intentionally," he replied, "but it comes to mind on a regular basis, about the same as it always has since '68. I must have nightmares about it from time to time, because my wife says I'll scream or bark orders in my sleep. I don't remember any of the dreams, only the thoughts and visions that pop up when I'm doing something else. It's always been worse on vacation, so I've made lots of excuses to avoid trips or have to cut them short because of work. At first, my wife used to put up a fight, but eventually she gave up the cause of having me relax."

At this point, I noticed that Jay was getting visibly upset. He didn't seem to be aware of it, but he began to wring his hands and then squeezed each hand with the other and slid it toward his fingertips. It looked as if he was drying his hands by wiping away a liquid. I wondered for a moment if this was some sort of ritual he engaged in to relax or a motor sequence associated with a memory. (I later learned it was a recurring behavior related to trying to wipe blood off his hands.) I thought it would be best to back off from this line of questioning to give him time to regroup and calm down. I thought that perhaps the two hours might be too much for him and wondered if we should stop early. I decided to change the subject for the moment to see how he would react.

"What kind of work did you do?" I asked next. "I was always pretty good with math," Jay replied, seemingly relieved by the change of subject, "so I went to college on the GI Bill and got a degree in business accounting. I bounced around at different jobs for a few years and then got hired at a petroleum company. Just retired last August after 40 years on the job—started as a clerk and worked my way up to chief operating officer." "Was it a difficult job?" I asked. "The work wasn't difficult, but it did keep me busy, always something to do, averaged 50–60 hours a week except for my two-week vacation every year. Hardly ever sick, put my kids through college, took care of my parents, and gave the family a good life. The Marines taught me discipline, taught me not to be afraid of hard work, and it paid off."

I could see his expression of pride and satisfaction, and I said, "I bet everyone is really proud of you." He teared up as he sat in silence. It was also becoming clear that his career had served multiple purposes—taking care of others, social status, identity, and, most importantly for our work, distraction.

"Would you call yourself a workaholic?" I asked, and a big smile came across his face. "I've been accused of that," he replied. This moniker was both a source of pride and served the purpose of keeping him in exile from his inner emotional world. I also noted how quickly his emotions could swing from sad to happy and back again. Jay spent the next half hour telling me stories about his family and career. This served our bonding while providing me with information about him that I would need for our work. When I noticed our time was up, I told him how much I had enjoyed meeting him and my interest in continuing our work. He said he would like to see me again as well, so we scheduled an appointment. Jay bounced up and left the office.

FURTHER REFLECTIONS

Happiness is the cessation of suffering.
THICH NHAT HANH

I found myself sitting with the immensity of the experiences and emotions Jay had carried within him for half a century. He had survived by not letting his fears and anxieties catch up with him by keeping on the move, staying distracted, and keeping immersed in the external world to avoid his traumatic memories. I wondered what he was thinking as he drove home. Was he deciding that these emotions were better left alone? Was Jay pulled off to the side of the road, overwhelmed with memories he could barely endure? Would he return for the next appointment? All of these thoughts passed through my mind as I stared at the chair he had been sitting in minutes before. I can attest to the fact that all of these are possible outcomes from a first therapy session, and I've experienced each of them over the years.

I reached for my computer to see if there was any information about the July Two ambush Jay had described. I discovered a Wikipedia page on Operation Buffalo that described the ambush which decimated the ranks of the Marines—in fact, more Marines were lost that day than on any other day in history. I began to have flashbacks of my own memories of the Vietnam War—not of combat, but of hearing the body count of American soldiers every night on the evening news; the protests that divided the nation; friends that went to Vietnam whole, but returned in pieces. Unlike the admiration and appreciation expressed for combat veterans today, Vietnam veterans returned to criticism and ridicule from antiwar protestors and absorbed the anger related to an unpopular war. This led many of them to withdraw from society, only connect with other vets, or bury their feelings and experiences deep inside themselves.

Jay's entire adult life had been influenced and shaped by his unresolved trauma. I imagined that Jay had a great deal of pain associated with that battle but feared that his loyalty to the Marines and his appreciation of his military service might block him from being able to discuss it openly. If Jay continued therapy, I would have to make a point of having him teach me as much as he could about his experience of being a Marine and of the battles he fought in. This would serve multiple purposes. The first would be to establish a bond and common vocabulary with which to discuss these painful experiences. A second would be to show him that I wasn't afraid to take a deep dive into his past and that he didn't have to protect me from his trauma. A third reason relates to the information processing involved in the dissociation of traumatic experiences. The more we avoid reflecting on painful or frightening memories, the more the avoidance is paired by our primitive brain with survival. In other words, we repeatedly avoid and survive until we condition ourselves into behaving as if the dissociation is absolutely necessary.

How might Porges's polyvagal theory apply to my work with Jay? In the weeks to come, I would have to assess Jay's ability to regulate his arousal and see if he was able to move through states of withdrawal, activation, and connection with others. What happened to his body when he had these memories? Did they put him into a frozen state of activation, or would he be able to combine them with active engagement with the memories? Might he be a good candidate for EMDR, systematic desensitization, or other techniques that could help his healing?

Almost all treatments for PTSD rely on exposure and response prevention—reexperiencing and confronting the trauma without denial or dissociation. Focusing on trauma allows for more conscious, cortical, left-hemisphere involvement with the memories and allows increased associated processing. Jay had carried this burden and struggled with his symptoms for almost half a century. In some cases, clients don't show for a second session and won't even answer my calls. Jay showing up next week would say a lot about him, his courage, and his readiness to heal. He would have to fight this internal battle between now and our next session. It's one thing to agree to meet with a therapist to satisfy your friend and doctor—it's another thing to be ready to do the work. After one session, all I had were questions, which is appropriate at the beginning of a therapeutic relationship.

I was so pleased to find Jay in my waiting room the following week filled with determination and ready to get down to work. He was a true Marine!

CHAPTER 11

TAMING DEMONS

Of all ghosts the ghosts of our old loves are the worst.
ARTHUR CONAN DOYLE

We are all inhabited by demons. Some have a deep species history—large fanged predators and monsters that hide beneath our beds. Others arise from personal experience—wrapped in memories of the enraged parent, a pedophile priest, or the sadistic teacher. Our demons are reflected in the nightmares of our childhood, the gods and devils of our religions, and the apocalyptic themes that fill our media. Although a similar race of demons resides within all of us, they feel so intensely personal that we tremble, isolated and alone when their shadows appear.

Some of my demons reflect the rage, violence, and frustrations I witnessed during childhood in the world around me. Others carry a message of my own lack of value, unlovability, and shame. I now know that everyone I grew up around was populated by their own demons. They found expression in anger, bad behavior, physical illness, compulsive behaviors, and nightmares, as they did in me. I learned that if you can't name your own demons, you see them in those around you and blame others for your suffering. My world, like yours, offered all the usual distractions and addictions—television, food, drugs, shopping, gambling, and so on, all ways to lose myself by "killing" time.

A central focus of psychotherapy is to guide your clients to battle and defeat their demons. Being a guide for this process is only possible if you have faced and battled your own demons. If you have yet to do this, you should know that domesticating your demons requires you to stop running and let them catch you. It's much the same as standing up to a bully who has been making your life miserable and taking away their power over you. Find the courage to turn away from all the distractions—stop overworking, put down the drink, get off social media—and turn to face what's chasing you. This is where you go into the fight mode of your sympathetic nervous system, and go toe-to-toe with whatever has been pursuing you. **This is the heroic battle of myth, how we become the alphas of our inner worlds and the CEO of our lives.** This is the only way to domesticate the demons that keep us hiding in the shadows of our own existence. Don't confuse fighting with violence; sometimes courage takes the form of passive resistance and holding your ground in the face of injustice.

UNIVERSAL SUFFERING

To live is to suffer, to survive is to find
some meaning in the suffering.
FRIEDRICH NIETZSCHE

Many of our clients are all too aware of their inner demons and describe them in different ways. My client Greg described his experience this way: "There is something inside of me screaming, trapped, and suffering. It's been incubating in my gut forever. It wants to break out, to explode. Sometimes it is quiet and distant. Other times it's intolerable and all I can do is get in my car and drive fast to try to outrace it. Sometimes I can, for a while, but it eventually catches up with me. I remember when I was a kid that I had this feeling very often. I would walk until I couldn't walk anymore, or run track until it was so dark I was running blind. It's always felt like a part of me but also bigger than my physical body and older than my age, like it was here before I was born and will be here after I'm gone."

As I learned more about evolution, biology, and the mind, I began to accept the fact that we experience far more than can be accounted for by our individual experiences. That our brains are social organs suggests that we attune and communicate with others at far deeper levels than everyday experience leads us to believe. I'm not speaking of telepathic powers, but something deeper and more primitive. While I don't believe we can communicate specific thoughts to each other through the ether, I do believe that we communicate with each other across space and time through emotional resonance, nonverbal gestures, and epigenetic signaling.

The psychiatrist Gabor Maté tells a story, as it was told to him by his mother. She described how, as a small child, he would have fits of crying that lasted for hours. As the days went by, his mother grew increasingly concerned and decided to call the doctor to see what was wrong. This took place in Hungary during the Nazi occupation of the 1940s as Hitler's gears turned at full speed. His mother, like all the Jewish inhabitants of Eastern Europe, lived in constant fear for their lives. One day, she was so certain that she was about to be arrested by the Nazis, she gave her son away to a stranger she met on the street, but fortunately soon got him back. When she reached the doctor on the phone and told him what was wrong, he said that he would certainly make a house call but thought she should know, "All of my Jewish babies are crying."

How misguided we are to think that children have to be told what is happening in order to feel what is going on around them. How many times have I been told by parents that their children's problems can't be due to their impending divorce because they haven't yet broken the news to them? How many spouses have told me that their partner has no idea that they're having an affair? How many of us suffer from the addiction, stress, and trauma of someone close to us?

Like the Jewish babies of Nazi-occupied Europe, we all resonate with the hearts, minds, and bodies of those around us. Over the course of our lives, we accumulate this kind of pain and can carry it for as long as we live. It is expressed, as Dr. Maté describes, as vulnerability to emotional stress, psychological symptoms, and being afraid of the world. It is also carried as anxiety, depression, or a sense of impending doom. Therapists spend a great deal of time trying to find the root causes of our physical and emotional disorders, as they should. But I think we should expand the search beyond the lifetime of the individual to their family, history, and culture. These variables should be seen as potentially central to someone's struggles.

A century ago, my family, like so many others, came across the ocean with the clothes on their backs, for the opportunities that did not exist in their native lands. What they discovered in the new world were horrible living conditions, inhumane working environments, prejudice, and danger from every direction. I grew up surrounded by these people who suffered injustices and chronic stress, and often died young and broken. They were ground up in factories that made ammunition, clothes, and toys and from building the skyscrapers, bridges, and subways of New York City. All of these things are in my mind, heart, and blood, although none of them can be found in the *DSM*. They are not recognized as traumas, but I can't be understood without knowing them, nor can I understand myself.

I can use these lived and inherited experiences as points of reference and empathy when connecting with others.

I keep in mind the prejudice and hatred southern Italians faced, both in Italy and in America, when I try to understand the racial hatred those of African descent have to endure. The small doses of prejudice I have experienced that have caused me pain serve as a window to understand those whose ancestors have been tortured, enslaved, and murdered.

The poet Robert Bly famously said that there is much suffering in nature. He was referring to the fact that, as animals, we have always struggled for survival, and that there are winners and losers. Primitive hunters felt the pain of the prey they had to kill and performed sacrifices in their honor. The Buddha said that all of life is suffering. We suffer because we desire for life to be other than it is and fear death despite its inevitability. Psychotherapy is often tasked with the job of relieving suffering, dispelling anxiety, and managing anger.

Who are we when we stop and take the time to ask? I've always believed that answering this question is a central goal of psychotherapy. As a therapist, you must be grounded in your humanity and aware of your own suffering. **The greatest gifts you can give to a client are your presence, your ear, and your vulnerability.**

THE THERAPIST'S DILEMMA

To learn to be a healer you must learn to mix
suffering with discipline and imagination.
ROBERT LOWELL

By this point in your career, it should not surprise you to discover that those of us who seek to heal others are on a secret mission to heal ourselves. As I discussed in *The Making of a Therapist*, it is common to find that those of us in the helping professions grew up in families where we played the role of diplomat, took care of others, or learned to defer our needs to those who claimed our attention. The demons that arise from such childhoods often carry the message to stay in the background, ignore your needs, and don't ask for anything for yourself.

From time to time, life provides us with an opportunity to confront these demons head on. Each time, there is a choice of moving into or retreating from the challenge; I've done both, many times. One example in my own life was when I was applying to graduate school, when the fear of rejection encouraged me to apply only to safe schools or avoid the process altogether. In this case, the demons whispered to me the story of my unworthiness, and how I would amount to nothing.

When I was writing my first book, other demons distracted me with imagined humiliating reviews and criticism. I was haunted by thoughts like, "What makes you think anyone is interested in what you think?" or "All of your ideas are nonsense." Perhaps my biggest demon to date emerged when I realized I only felt safe in relationships where I was the caretaker, too frightened to let anyone take care of me. I was certain that I would be abandoned if I was needy, weak, or vulnerable. This time, I had to come face to face with a demon in the form of a gargoyle, so close in fact that I could feel its hot breath. In the end, it was just another demon to tame; I'm sure there are more to come.

Each of these situations brought forth a set of emotions that converted a normal rite of passage into a referendum on my value as a person. No one else noticed these dramas but me, yet my inner drama blew them up into life-and-death struggles. They exposed cracks in my character and personality where the demons could gain entry and lead me to shrink from the three faces of my shame—fear of failure, humiliation, and abandonment. Facing, battling, and domesticating our demons, rather than shrinking from the challenge, allows us to live in a safer and calmer inner world. It also prepares us for the battle the next time another demon rears its ugly head. If we engage in this heroic journey, we feel calmer, safer, and more at home within ourselves. This empowerment allows us to go even deeper within ourselves and become better guides for our clients.

When I work with a client, I start by imagining the young child within them, no matter their actual age. I use my own emotions to feel more deeply what might be going on inside them. I attempt to surrender to their experience, their needs, their suffering, and stay open to whatever my imagination offers up to consciousness. I try to stay connected with this imaginary child in my own inner experience and keep them in my heart.

Whatever arises in this internal imaginary incubator I take as potentially valuable information. Whether it is relevant to the client can never be fully known until tested. Despite the inevitable difference between us, our emotions usually serve as a common language of connection.

I don't believe this introspective-imaginative strategy works because of our intellect—almost the opposite. It works to the degree to which we can jump off our intellect onto our emotions, intuitions, and bodily sensations. Although there are clients for whom this strategy doesn't work, I always give it a try. If I can connect with someone at this more primal, nonverbal level, it is a doorway to the trust required to make more challenging interventions. Many clients are too afraid and defended to connect emotionally with their therapist. They insist on keeping us at a distance and may not even realize they are doing it. I've had a few clients like this tell me that they have been fired by therapists because they were "treatment resistant." Sometimes, diving into a shared imaginative and emotional space can help me find a way to help a client, while other times it fails. This is why it is so important to have many different strategies in your toolbox.

THE HOPE FOR PROGRESS—WITHOUT ANXIETY

You're braver than you believe, and stronger than
you seem, and smarter than you think.

A. A. MILNE

The philosopher Arthur Schopenhauer famously said, "To understand something is to be delivered from it." Meaning that if you can label a problem and understand its mechanisms, it will no longer be a problem. This belief is applied to therapy by many clients and therapists. They hope that the right diagnosis and etiological theory, coupled with the clarity of these insights, and even figuring out who did wrong to them, will allow them to circumvent the terror of facing and defeating their demons. "Now that I know what's wrong with me, I can take on the challenges at work. I can express my feelings to my family. I can stand up to my oppressors, and say what's on my mind." Taking it out into the world will be a piece of cake.

In my experience, this rarely happens. It is true that a clear understanding of the problem serves as a proper road map for navigating the challenges ahead. Rehearsing interactions in therapy creates sensory-motor maps that can help us along, and expressing the emotions to a therapist can break down neural and psychological dissociations that help us to stay conscious when the going gets tough. However, these are like the preparations we make to go on a challenging adventure, not the adventure itself. I have found it helpful to prepare a client for this reality early in the therapeutic process. It is helpful, when appropriate, to warn them of the emotional challenges they will soon confront. This kind of preparation, for some, can serve as a form of stress inoculation. Know that some will flee your office and go in search of a therapist that can promise an easier way forward. But more seasoned clients appreciate the warning and remember it when it is time to convert their learning in therapy into the experiments in living required for change.

Conscious awareness is only the tip of the iceberg of brain/mind functioning that involves all of our sensory, motor, vestibular, emotional, and biochemical processing. You have probably experienced the internal battle of whether to exercise or not, jump off the diving board, or run for 5 or 10 miles. You can think about it forever, but doing it is a full-body experience, which can only be described in inadequate ways. The neurologist Oliver Sacks discovered, after spending weeks in bed following a major quadriceps surgery, that he had forgotten how to walk. He couldn't think himself into walking, nor could he will it to happen. Two stout physiotherapists lifted him up and walked him about until his brain and legs could reestablish connection and remember the automatic movements they had performed since childhood. Top-down learning is only half the battle; bottom-up learning is just as critical to healing.

TOXIC PERFECTIONISM

Perfectionism is the voice of the oppressor.
ANNE LAMOTT

Because we are social beings, those who have cared for us and made us feel seen, as well as those who shamed us or made us feel invisible, continue to live within us. They live in our minds, brains, and bodies and either help us to navigate life or impede our progress via their surrogates, our internal demons. Because of this, individual therapy often takes place in a room crowded with others from the client's life, as well as the therapist's. In therapy, we confront and negotiate with the people within us; our parents as they were decades ago, the teacher who told us we wouldn't amount to anything, the man who raped us, the woman who hurt us, the fathers who abandoned us, and the mothers who died when we were too young.

Meanwhile, we are vigilantly focused on the minds of those around us—What are they thinking? What do they need? Do they like us? Are they dangerous? Our demons often become confused with the real people around us and appear in their form: Is this my husband or my abusive father? Is this my boss or the older sister who once tormented me? We have to somehow forge our own separate identity in spite of the fact that we are just a montage of those around us. It is a rare individual that stands out as unique, perhaps a more interesting montage—Steve Jobs, Bob Dylan, Barack Obama—than the norm. We may aspire to be like these people, yet most of us are made of more everyday stuff. Our montage of self has been orchestrated by social evolution. Being made up of those around us, past and present, and staying fixated on their needs guarantees the tribe a fabric of obligations and behavior that ensures its survival.

Although we think one of the tasks of therapy is assisting in the process of individuation, being woven into a social network is both a fact and a necessity. Perhaps what we are actually doing is more like internal family therapy—first discovering areas of misunderstanding, conflict, and misattunement among those who populate our inner world, discovering the parts of us that have been marginalized or scapegoated, and helping them to find their voice. When we finally arrive at the notion of who we are, our true identity, we will discover that it still consists of the bits and bobs of others. This perspective doesn't diminish us; it may simply be a clearer description of what we are made of.

I spoke with a client whose mother was the center of her emotional life up until her death about a dozen years ago. Since then, she had been isolated, alone, and afraid to take personal or professional risks. When I asked her how she experienced her mother today, all these years after her death, her response was, "She's dead. She's gone. I don't have her anymore." This was not the response I expected, and I struggled to understand what this must be like. I reflected on how much I relied on the memories of my parents and grandparents, and how they live in me, especially during difficult times. I've felt their presence inside of me so many times and imagined them next to me, smiling and putting their hands on my back in support. I think about my mother's dedication to raising me and my father's work ethic—all of these feel like solid internal blocks that fortify me against the challenges I've encountered. While my grandparents' deaths were terribly sad, there is a continuity of experience that is more powerful than their death, because I still feel them inside me.

This interaction with my client helped me to understand the distance between our experience and how much I wanted to help her gain the kind of connection with her mother that I have with my grandparents. Turning away from her memories left her empty, bereft of the love that could be serving as the foundation of her future. I began to work with her by having her write stories about her mother and focusing on the feelings evoked by the stories. This served as a vehicle to suggest that her mother was certainly alive in her, which is one of the benefits of having a social brain. In the past she had coped with her mother's death by putting her out of her mind and reacting to sad memories by drinking, shopping, and overeating. I encouraged her to grasp these memories and tolerate the negative feelings long enough to get to the positive emotions of love and connection that were hiding just beyond them. I wanted her to exhume her mother's memory, take control of it, internalize their intimacy, and connect it with her day-to-day life.

While I will never question the perfectionism of a brain surgeon at work, perfectionism can also be the visible tip of an iceberg of shame, driven by feelings of being unworthy and unlovable. Being perfect in these cases is an attempt to avoid creating any evidence of these internal fears and the expectation of being shunned by the group, which, for social animals like ourselves, equals death.

It's a cliché in the business world that "the great is the enemy of the good." Many forms of this sentiment have been expressed by the likes of Shakespeare, Voltaire, and Confucius. In everyday terms, it refers to the fact that seeking greatness or perfection can get in the way of doing something of value. I've known students who never get around to writing their dissertation because nothing they do can live up to their fantasies. This is also true for writing a book, trying out for a team, or sending your screenplay to an agent. You can imagine in all of these instances that aspiring to the great and not being able to accept anything less can keep you from attaining what you are capable of. Ultimately, most people who create something great spent considerable time failing, and doing something that was good, before they reached their goal.

Perfectionism, and the inability to tolerate anything else, is usually a sign of a defense that can stall your ability to move forward in all aspects of life. All expressions of this defense stem from a basic lack of acceptance of the self and the desire to keep our imperfection hidden from others.

This is likely why winning a Nobel Prize or dating the most handsome man in the world doesn't help—these are external solutions for an internal dilemma. There is never enough external recognition to make up for self-loathing; never enough fame or awards for feeling unlovable. This is why so many who achieve fame soon become disillusioned and suffer even more than before.

Just as there are those who are unable to benefit from therapy, many students are unable to learn from clinical training. There are always students who are too broken and defended to benefit from feedback and supervision. They go to therapy themselves to tick the box but don't or can't do the work. I personally lost so many good learning opportunities because I couldn't tolerate being wrong. It took me decades to develop enough confidence in myself to accept my ignorance, listen to teachers, and be satisfied with incremental steps toward mastery. Perfectionism can destroy everything, take the life out of living, and take the joy and adventure out of learning. I wish I had the wisdom back then to be in therapy prior to the beginning of my training.

LEARNING TO LEARN

He who is not everyday conquering some
fear has not learned the secret of life.

RALPH WALDO EMERSON

One of the experiences that characterized my childhood was my father's expectation that I would know how to do things I was never taught to do. He would ask me to do something, identify a tool, or answer a question with which I was unfamiliar, and then criticize me for failing. (As I learned later, he was passing on the parenting he had been subject to.) As a result, I grew up feeling unintelligent, dim-witted, and, in his words, "Not too bright!" The result was an overattention to understanding and learning that has both helped and hindered me for decades. One of the primary ways in which these experiences got in my way was the shame connected to not knowing. When with teachers, I was so embarrassed about not knowing what they knew that I made it very hard for them to teach and for me to learn. I tried to convince them that I already knew what they were teaching me and that I didn't really need them to show me, despite the fact that I invested all of my energy, time, and resources in being in their classes. I was just too ashamed of my ignorance.

This paradoxical behavior makes no sense based on the surface information, but complete sense when seen in the light of the deep narrative of my psychological and emotional history. The experiment in living, still occurring to this day, is to enter a state of mind that is open to new learning without the soundtrack of shame blaring in the background. I remember with delight attending a lecture by Robert Sapolsky and feeling palpitations of excitement from the clarity of his words and his brilliant articulation of biological processes. Reflecting on the lecture, I realized that I had not had one moment of self-awareness or shame—I had totally surrendered to the learning experience provided by a wonderful teacher. Fortunately, this experiment in living has been repeated numerous times since.

One of the hardest lessons I've had to learn is to find strength in vulnerability and the difference between the two. Strength is often fear in disguise. The analysts sometimes call this counterphobic behavior, which leads someone with a fear of heights to become a skydiver or a claustrophobic to take a ride in a submarine. In my case, this led me to cover insecurities about my own intelligence by acting like a know-it-all. Learning to be comfortable in the position of a student—which, incidentally, didn't happen until I was in my late 20s—was a great boon. I found that making myself vulnerable to their evaluation and criticism didn't result in being shamed and humiliated. Rather, I found that my teachers appreciated my interest, enthusiasm, and dedication to learning. And when I was criticized, I could take it without being crushed, think about it, and learn more because of it.

CHAPTER 12

THE EXECUTIVE BRAINS

Freedom is control in your own life.
WILLY NELSON

In *The Making of a Therapist,* we covered the importance of formulating and utilizing a clinical case conceptualization to help guide our psychotherapeutic work. In this chapter, I would like to share with you a conceptualization of executive functioning you might use to understand your clients' abilities to navigate their day-to-day lives.

In clinical psychology, the term "executive functioning" is generally only used (1) when discussing the impact of significant brain damage, or (2) when attempting to diagnose the cause of academic difficulties. It encompasses a wide range of skills including attentional control, problem-solving, and abstract abilities. According to the *Oxford English Dictionary,* the word "executive" (related to "execute") has been used as far back as the 17th century meaning "to carry into practical effect"—in other words, the ability to take an idea, wish, or intention and make it so. This was the generally accepted working definition of executive functioning I was taught in school, and still in use today. But for the most part, Western psychology turned it into a purely cognitive, top-down function having everything to do with rational thought and nothing to do with emotion, self-awareness, or empathy for others.

In parallel with the bias toward the cognitive aspects of executive functioning was the attempt to localize executive functioning within the prefrontal cortex. Both of these biases remain strong despite considerable evidence to the contrary. Any of us who have worked with clients soon learn that deficits of social and emotional functioning play just as powerful a role in executive functioning as cognitive abilities.

Those of us who work in organizations immediately see the inadequacy of a strictly cognitive model of executive functioning. A person's intellectual abilities and knowledge of their industry might get them into a position of leadership. But being an effective executive also requires well-developed emotional and social functioning. It is the combination of emotional, social, and cognitive abilities that, in the long run, differentiate success from failure in bringing your ideas "into practical effect." This is equally true for those with brain damage or ADHD as it is for corporate executives.

The problem with the cognitive definition of executive functioning is that it harkens back to a time before neurologists realized that there is no "cold cognition." What this means is that the neuronal systems that organize our cognitive, somatic, social, and emotional experiences are inextricably interwoven. The failure of an adolescent to perform well on measures of executive functioning usually doesn't tell us if they are struggling in school because of emotional challenges or ADHD. This narrow cognitive perspective on human functioning is why so many neuropsychological reports do little more than take up space in a client's file. **Executive functioning is a whole brain and body experience and needs to be understood in the context of a person's entire being.**

IN SEARCH OF THE SOURCE

You must have confidence in your competence.

ELIJAH CUMMINGS

The vast majority of our bodily and mental functions are on automatic pilot. Under normal circumstances, we pay virtually no attention to breathing, walking, talking, and thousands of other complex processes. We can drive a car safely (and mindlessly) for hours while listening to music or having a conversation. All of this automaticity allows us to focus our conscious attention on just a small fraction of what is actually happening. We spend the first years of life learning to bond and attach to those around us, how to navigate our environments, and where we fit in the social order. Cognitive executive functioning, as usually defined, comes around years later and rests upon all prior social and emotional learning.

Neurology's early push to localize functions to specific areas of the brain has led both to progress and stagnation. Ever since Broca designated an area of the left frontal cortex as the speech center, the search has been on for the center of all other functions. It turned out that each area of the brain is part of a number of complex systems. For higher-order processes like executive functioning, the search for a center is especially misleading. Add to this the cultural assumptions about the supremacy of cognitive functioning (I think, therefore I am), and it is easy to see how Western scientists have come to assume that there is a little guy in our head (the homunculus) who is pushing buttons and shifting levers.

The central dogma of executive functioning is that it is located in the frontal lobes. And there is no doubt that the correct crossword answer for a seven-letter word describing "the region of the brain that controls executive functioning" would be "F-R-O-N-T-A-L." Fortunately, the impulse to localize functions to one area of the brain is being undermined. We are moving from a focus on localization to exploring the neurodynamics of interwoven neural systems. This is allowing the notion of executive functioning to expand from purely cognitive functioning to include interpersonal and emotional abilities such as attunement, empathy, and affect regulation. While the frontal lobes are central players in executive functioning, it turns out that executive functioning is a group effort.

The truth about executive functioning is that it is a full-participation brain function reliant on multiple neural systems as well as our brains' ability to connect with our physical and social worlds. Think about the executive functioning that it takes to be a successful psychotherapist—you not only have to attend to, organize, and remember a great deal of information, you also have to develop a meaningful connection with your client and find a way to communicate your thoughts in a way which allows them to be understood and accepted. As we all know (or should know), psychotherapy is much more than just a cognitive task.

THREE INTERACTING EXECUTIVE SYSTEMS

Teamwork is a strategic decision.
PATRICK LENCIONI

While we are at the early stages of developing a neurodynamic model of executive functioning, I would like to share the model I use with my psychotherapy and executive coaching clients. I believe this model accounts for many of the aspects of executive functioning that are usually left unaddressed by cognitive and neuropsychologists. My proposal is that there are at least three executive systems that interact in a dynamic balance. Further, all three networks are in executive control of different aspects of functioning and need to integrate with one another for optimal executive functioning.

The first executive system is centered in the most primitive areas of the brain, including the amygdala and regions of the brain stem. This amygdala network, which we share with reptiles and other mammals, is responsible for our moment-to-moment survival reactions and drives our physiological responses to the environment. The amygdala is an organ of appraisal that guides us in making basic approach-avoidance decisions. It is the source of our anxieties, tensions, and fears and guides us toward what we have experienced as safe and away from what has proven to be dangerous.

It is when this primitive executive system is overactive that we experience anxiety disorders, panic attacks, and PTSD. In a dangerous situation, the amygdala executive immediately takes over and inhibits our other two executive systems until the danger has passed. In a sense, it maintains veto power over our actions in the face of later-evolving systems of executive control. This process of invoking veto power over the other systems is sometimes called amygdala hijack.

The second executive system is organized by regions of the frontal and parietal lobes and the fiber bundles that connect them. This system is primarily responsible for navigating the environment, problem solving, and abstract reasoning. This is also the system most people are referring to when they speak about the executive functioning limited to the prefrontal cortex. During evolution, the frontal lobes became specialized to process timing, sequencing, and holding a memory for future consequences of actions in the present moment. Meanwhile, the parietal lobes evolved to develop maps of external and internal space and to integrate these maps to use for spatial and imaginal navigation. It is in the frontal and parietal lobes where we find the mirror neurons that allow us to attune with and learn from others through imitation. Together, the parietal and frontal lobes create our sense of space and time and navigate it with minimal conscious attention. When this system is damaged or disrupted, we experience difficulties in engaging in functional sequences of events, navigating space, and disturbances in consciousness. In other words, we have difficulty in executing functional abilities.

The third executive system is centered around a group of structures along the middle regions of the brain called the default mode network (DMN). First detected in research subjects between experimental tasks, it was later discovered to be a coherent group of interconnected structures. Subsequent research discovered that the DMN becomes activated during reflection, empathic attunement, daydreaming, and imagination. The DMN is involved with our awareness and understanding of ourselves and others and our capacity to create an internal world and use it as an imaginal space within which we can reflect on real-world problems, rehearse solutions, and access our creativity. Because the amygdala can inhibit both the parietal-frontal and the DMN executives, stress and anxiety decrease our cognitive, emotional, and social executive abilities.

Think for a moment about these structures of the executive brain as they might relate to a business executive. A successful CEO is usually judged first and foremost on the ability to understand her area of expertise and make good decisions based on a deep understanding of a specific industry (second executive). In addition, she needs to be able to regulate her arousal, mood, and temper in order to interact appropriately with others (first executive). Finally, she has to be able to remain self-possessed, keep her own counsel, and understand the feelings, needs, and motivations of those around her (third executive).

In my coaching work with executives, everyone I work with has a highly functional second executive, knows their industry, and excels in the cognitive challenges of their work. If there are problems in these areas, more appropriate assistance will come from other industry experts and not myself. The problems I am confronted with are generally in the areas of the first and third executive systems. On one hand, people who struggle with anxiety, depression, and difficulty regulating their arousal and emotions (first executive) need to understand and deal with dysregulations of their physiology and affective arousal. Emotional dysregulation and instability will keep an intelligent and competent executive (or any of us for that matter) from being able to stay on task, keep problems in perspective, and sustain focus on a goal. They will be sabotaged by their own emotional dyscontrol and fear of being judged by others. Another group will struggle with their ability to empathize, attune with, and understand the perspective of those they work with and for (third executive). For these individuals, our work will focus on attunement, empathy, and social skills requiring the involvement of the DMN.

While I believe this model of executive functioning can be helpful across a wide range of clients and situations, there is an even deeper and more urgent use of this model addressing the ubiquitous problem of internet overuse, abuse, and addiction. We will now shift our focus to explore the potential impact of the internet on the development, functioning, and interconnection among these three executive systems.

EXECUTIVE FUNCTIONING AND THE INTERNET

The Internet is a big distraction.
RAY BRADBURY

The ubiquity of the internet early in life and in the day-to-day lives of adult businesspeople may be having a profound effect on executive functioning. How might excessive internet use, or what might be labeled as internet addiction, impact the development and functioning of the three executive systems?

Beginning with the first executive system, we know that the development of the regulatory systems of the amygdala begins with the early development of its connectivity with the prefrontal cortex. The descending networks from the prefrontal cortex to the amygdala are built by early attachment relationships.

Optimizing this process requires attentive and attuned caretakers to link with the child's brain and move them in a timely manner from states of dysregulation to reregulation. In research with mothers and children, it was found that distracted and misattuned mothers often had children with insecure attachment styles. This means that their amygdala would become dysregulated, resulting in autonomic hyperarousal and decreased self-regulation. The degree to which secure attachment and emotional regulation are established early in life will also influence the activation and ongoing development of the other two executive systems.

There is little doubt that excessive screen focus will take any parent's attention away from their child, and everyone else for that matter. It is impossible to miss the day-to-day examples of children looking for their parents' attention while parents are attending to phones, tablets, and laptops. The research has shown us that parents who created secure attachment in their children were able to quickly notice and attend to their child's needs and were able to return to their own activities once the child returned to play. Of course, screens aren't the only distraction in a parent's world, but they may certainly be the most seductive and the only one engineered by social engineers to capture and hold our attention.

As children grow into adolescents and adults, it appears that the amount of screen time correlates with a variety of amygdala-related functions that result in higher levels of arousal, anxiety, and depression. One of the most interesting findings was that when adolescents troll on social media (look at the pages of others without posting), they don't exhibit any immediate negative effects. However, they do experience an increase in anxiety and depression about 30 minutes after disengaging. The theory as to why this occurs is that the process of social comparison takes a while to have negative effects on neurochemical and anatomical structures. Because social media has become a personal public relations platform, trolling the internet likely creates a subjective state where we look at the lives of others and feel as if we are missing out or not measuring up. As they say in AA, we compare our insides to other people's outside and feel shame, anticipate rejection, and feel depressed. The kids just call it FOMO.

In addition, the amount and nature of information we are bombarded with, and the expanding number of things we have to take care of results in a chronically high level of stress that undermines our sense of comfort, physical safety, and self-possession. Many of the high school and college students I work with have a constant sense of being behind where they should be by their age. Given that their heroes are teenage media influencers and 25-year-old billionaires, they feel that by 20, they have already fallen behind. What a different world it is than the one I grew up in, where high school and college weren't about success and money, but were times of exploration, articulating your dreams, and of course, sex, drugs, and rock and roll.

Anxiety, stress, and time pressure are the enemies of creativity and exploration. A significant contributor to this phenomenon is the fact that the high levels of amygdala activation triggered by stress serve to inhibit processing in the other two executive systems. In other words, the anticorrelational nature of the executive systems causes anxiety to inhibit navigation of both the external world of the second

executive system and the internal and social worlds organized by the third. To whatever degree excessive internet use
stimulates pressure and anxiety via social shame, information overload, or functional problems from addictive gaming,
the development of thinking, feeling, and connecting may be
compromised.

The second executive system of the parietal and frontal
lobes evolved to navigate a three-dimensional world through
time and incorporate our tools as part of the self. For these and
other reasons, we have not only adapted our digital devices
to ourselves, they have become extensions of our experience of self. I was fascinated when an art professor told me
that she was having to teach incoming students how to use a
pencil. She is finding that many students entering college to
study art have only used graphics programs and have never
drawn anything in the analog world. I was surprised by how
something as basic as using a pencil, something I learned as
a small child, is a skill (like writing in cursive) that may soon
become extinct.

The parietal-frontal systems are shaped by our interactions with the environment and then come to shape how we
are able to interact with the world. In a sense, our brains take
the shape of the environment in which we live; we become
what we do. If we consistently interact with devices, we will
gain certain skills while losing others. The big question is,
what are the costs of these trade-offs? An example that is
becoming a cause of increasing concern is how the infinite
availability of internet pornography will impact sexual development and intimate relationships. A number of my students
have told me that they are struggling to decrease their pornography use because of its impact on their relationships.

THE SHALLOWS

I have no fear of depths and a great fear of shallow living.
ANAÏS NIN

One of the ways in which the second executive adapts to the environment is the way in which it deploys our attention. If we are sitting in a quiet, comfortable position, we can put all of our attention into the book we are reading and be transported into the world of our imagination. But if the dog starts barking, the kids come home from school, or someone puts on music, you will notice the depth of attention to reading decreases as it is spread across multiple points of focus. There is no right or wrong way to deploy attention; rather, it is a question of functional adaptation. It is highly adaptive to focus deeply when you are doing woodwork, playing with a child, or doing surgery. It is highly adaptive to widen your focus when you are alone in the woods listening for predators, or when you have multiple things on the stove that require proper sequencing and timing.

With the full penetration of the internet, we have now been conditioned to consistently check our phone, be simultaneously involved with multiple screens, and have an increasing number of tasks to do each day—from checking social media to returning text messages, to posting our dinner photos before we say, "Bon appetit." In other words, our attention is spread thin, and some are losing the ability to focus on the same topic for more than 20 seconds. Many of my students tell me that they no longer have the attention span to read the books and articles I assigned for class. Their scattered attentional capacities don't allow them to focus long enough to read an entire paragraph without checking messages or their Instagram account. Educators are struggling to figure out how to chunk information for the brain/screen, so they are packaging their lessons on videos and in fortune cookie–size bits of information. I suspect, however, there are some things, reading Shakespeare for instance, that may not be amenable to sound bites.

Attention and arousal are closely linked. The most basic level of attention is the orienting reflex. When we hear, see, or feel something unexpected we, like other animals, reflexively orient to it. This allows for the next step of appraising its value as something we should approach or avoid. When we orient, our autonomic nervous system goes on alert to deal with what might occur. We can also be activated in this way by internal processes, such as having something on our mind, a memory that we need to do something, or perhaps a pleasant or unpleasant feeling. These shifts of attention activate the amygdala and inhibit the other two executive systems, resulting in an interruption of sustained attention.

When our phones ring, buzz, or vibrate, we orient to them and experience arousal. Now that we have been conditioned to check our phones every 20–30 seconds, we now have internal alarms that interrupt our focus. Ultimately, companies such as Google, Facebook, and Instagram make their money by selling advertising. The more things you click on, and the more time you spend looking at your screen, the more money these companies make. This is why their social engineers are in the business of keeping you online instead of in your life. When apps designed to help us decrease our screen time are offered to the Apple store, they are turned down. Apple is not in the business of helping us have real lives.

There is another twist to the story, which is the covert relationship between the social engineers of Silicon Valley and our own amygdala. Let me explain: The amygdala's primary job is to protect us from danger, stress, and discomfort, so it subliminally directs us away from difficult situations and toward things that decrease our anxiety. In the primitive context in which it evolved, this meant staying away from predators and moving toward mates, food, and safe shelter. But in modern times, our contemporary brains have many more sources of stress and more complex ways of dealing with it. The same drives that made our ancestors avoid predators now push us to avoid paying bills, doing our homework, or making a difficult phone call. The amygdala steers us away from these tasks and toward Pokémon Go, Candy Crush, and net surfing.

THE EXILE FROM SELF

I know how men in exile feed on dreams.
AESCHYLUS

Addiction to the internet is the result of unbridled capitalism's collision with our evolutionary mandates to avoid discomfort. The social engineers know how to manipulate the amygdala to make us anxious when we are separated from our devices and how to make us experience their presence as soothing. The fact that we feel calmer when we are holding and looking at our phones, and more anxious when we aren't, reflects a global behavioral experiment. The outcome is completely by design and all driven by commerce.

The third executive system (or DMN) is most centrally involved with abilities associated with social cognition and our connection with others. It is also central to having a conscious experience of ourselves in imaginal space within the flow of time. The internet is designed and engineered to keep us engaged with it, in essence, to keep our parietal-frontal systems activated for as many hours of the day as possible. Because the DMN is generally anticorrelational with both the frontal-parietal and amygdala executive networks, when we are either preoccupied with a task or anxious and afraid, we are far less likely to have access to the following capacities linked to DMN functioning:

Self-awareness	Self-reflective capacities	Imagination
Mental time travel	Stimulus-independent thought	Autobiographical memory
Recognizing faces	Processing social relationships	Theory of mind
Creativity	Grasping moral dilemmas	Empathy

Activation in the DMN has been detected as early as two weeks after birth, forms a loose network around age seven, and begins to become functionally coherent during early adulthood. Its slow development and the variability we see across individuals in its functions suggests that its organization is highly dependent on experience. This is supported by findings that early trauma and maltreatment correlate with decreased functional connectivity and development of the DMN.

When children grow up within an internet ecosystem, there is a risk that the development of their DMNs will be inhibited. And given that we need the DMN for the kind of self-awareness to realize we are addicted, the addiction itself will block the victim from healing. As an example, the primitive executive of the amygdala may activate anxiety, leading to a conscious or unconscious awareness of that anxiety, causing us to reflexively reach for a device. The second executive would do the essential scanning and navigation to check the phone. It would be the DMN that would allow us to think, "Wait, why do I need my phone?" and be able to ask the more fundamental question, "Why am I anxious?"

The potential impact of internet addiction on the DMN is not just theoretical. A study of a group of adolescents who qualified as internet addicted showed decreases in the number of neurons in the anterior and posterior cingulate cortex and the insular cortex in the left hemisphere (Zhou et al., 2011). These areas are all processing hubs of the DMN that contribute to organizing attention, self-awareness, decision making, attachment, empathy, and emotional awareness. It does appear that some of the deficits we are seeing in internet-addicted people correspond to these underdeveloped brain regions.

The less DMN activation we have, the more we become human doings rather than human beings. In psychological research this has been called field dependence, a phenomenon seen in individuals with brain damage, anxiety disorders, and posttraumatic stress. As you might imagine, field dependence leads you to react to the environment with a minimum of reflection or free will, making you a perfect target for salesmen, con artists, and malevolent dictators. In addition, the addictive nature of the internet increases subcortical impulses and decreases executive control, which further serves to undermine the development of the DMN.

We have the challenge as therapists, educators, and human beings to take this threat to our consciousness and executive functioning seriously and regain control of our attention. Social engineers leverage our own amygdala against us to keep us scanning, swiping, clicking, and shopping. I feel we need to educate our clients about the threat to their development and help them learn how to develop their reflective and imaginative capacities. The capacity for self-awareness and self-possession may be more important now than ever.

CHAPTER 13

THE CHALLENGES AHEAD

The internet has been a boon and a curse for teenagers.

J. K. ROWLING

Since the publication of *The Making of a Therapist,* there have been many new challenges to both therapeutic practice and the culture at large. Perhaps the most important is the impact of the internet on brain development, social relatedness, and emotional well-being. I would say that now the majority of clients we see are, in one way or another, addicted to the internet. The impact and implications of internet addiction vary across age groups and need to be addressed separately with each of our clients.

A second challenge is how attachment-based parenting has changed the developmental landscape of recent generations. While the increased connection between parents and children has had many positive results, the effects on separation and individuation do not all seem positive. Instead of sending adolescents out into the world to learn from the school of hard knocks, many parents now forge the path for them, which may decrease their opportunities to build resilience.

Venturing out into the world has always been the best way for children and adolescents to test their nascent skills and abilities. But there is far less venturing forth these days—the world seems more dangerous, homes have become entertainment centers, and most adventures take place online. As a consequence, many younger adults come to therapy with the belief that being uncomfortable, experiencing stress, and feeling anxiety should always be avoided. A financial firm I consulted with was aghast when a 26-year-old brought his mother with him for a job interview. The mother was genuinely curious whether it would be best for her to join in the interview or to wait in the lobby, while her son passively looked on. While this may be an extreme case, it reflects attachment-based parenting in the absence of a plan for individuation. The belief that all stress is bad for healthy development has led to two consequences; children who break down at low levels of stress, and parents who can't tolerate their children's discomfort. A parade of tutors, test takers, and college admission scandals follow.

When we are first learning how to do anything complicated, we use lots of energy attending to each and every detail. The skills and abilities of being assertive, standing up to bullies, or presenting well during a job interview are learned. While we may be helped along by genetics, biology, and experience, all trial-and-error learning involves uncertainty, anxiety, and stress. When you first learn to drive, every behavior is conscious, second guessed, and scary. After a few weeks, you are not only driving but also listening to the radio, having conversations, and steering with one hand. If you are unable to tolerate the anxiety and stress involved in the process of learning, you will remain trapped behind the wall of your own fears. While early development depends upon close parental scaffolding, many of us seem to lack a model of how to increasingly dismantle this scaffolding so children can learn to explore their worlds.

Over the past decade, we have gotten our first glimpse of how the total penetration of screens into our lives is affecting how we think, feel, and relate to one another. This includes the first generation of children raised online while their parents are also online. Because the brain is a social organ, the introduction of a communication device into a relationship changes the dynamic connections among individuals. From the moment of birth and throughout our lives, our brains are built and regulated via social interactions. But with screens everywhere, attention is diverted and altered, a seemingly infinite amount of new information is added, and the primitive one-on-one connection that has evolved over millions of years is being altered. Research has shown that the mere presence of a phone turned upside down on a table impacts the social dynamics of those present. Whether this is a good thing or a bad thing, it is certain that screens, in all their forms, are here to stay.

As therapists, our job is to understand these changes and their impact on human experience, and learn how to modify treatment to account for their presence and impact. In this chapter, I would like to explore the impact of screens and the implications for our work as therapists. The topics I highlight are their impacts on child-rearing, attention, brain development, and mental health. These are big questions, and an exhaustive exploration is impossible, even in an entire book. My goal here is to raise the issues so you can include them in your thinking as you are assessing and treating your clients.

PARENTS, CHILDREN, AND SCREENS

Love is space and time measured by the heart.
PROUST

About a year ago, I had some free time between meetings and decided to find somewhere to have lunch. As I walked along an unfamiliar street, I noticed a small supermarket up ahead and decided to have a look. A few minutes later, sandwich in hand, I headed to a counter with stools facing out the front window. After I sat down, I noticed, just outside the store, tables and chairs that looked much more comfortable. As I was gathering up my things to relocate, I noticed something that made me sink back onto my stool. At an outside table, directly in front of me, was a mother sitting across from her one-year-old in a stroller. What stopped me in my tracks was the distressed look on the child's face as her mother picked up her phone.

I flashed to memories of the films I had seen of infants' reactions to their expressionless mothers ("still-face" experiments), and I was curious to see how this child would react to having her mother's face replaced with the back of a phone. The heavily tinted glass that separated us guaranteed I could observe them without being detected. The mother played her role perfectly, holding up the phone in front of her at an angle that, for her child, replaced her face with the back of her phone. At first, the baby looked interested in the phone and watchfully tracked her mother's hand movements as she swiped left and right, up and down. I set the stopwatch on my phone and set it in front of me so I could make notes about the timing of their interactions. At 15 seconds, the baby began to protest, rhythmically kicking her feet and letting out an occasional yell. It seemed clear that she was trying to capture her mother's attention. The mother, playing her role perfectly, proceeded to swipe, take a selfie, and what looked like adding a caption, and then posting it.

This continued until the 50-second mark, when the little one seemed to deflate. She suddenly became lethargic, looked about, and then hung her head limply down and to the left. After a while, she began to look up and around again. At 74 seconds, she oriented toward a bird hopping by, people passing, and the wind moving the colorful umbrellas overhead. One after another, they captured and then lost her attention.

Her face became strained, as if she was angry or had a stomachache. She began to shake her legs, let out an occasional yell, and looked up from time to time to see the back of the phone. At 103 seconds, she again looked deflated. At this point, I became aware of how deflated I felt watching her face. I also felt the urge to reach out and pick her up. My mind flashed to wondering how many times I might have ignored my own son in the same way.

At 157 seconds, her mother put down her phone and took a sip of her coffee. When she looked down at her baby, I could feel the relief in my own body, and the thought "Thank God" went through my mind. If this were my research project, I might have called it off. Now, at 176 seconds, the mother was trying to get the little one's attention, but her child no longer seemed interested. There were no visible responses to her words or gestures, just the baby's limp head hanging to the left and a blank stare. Was this intentional avoidance, a state of hopelessness, or exhaustion? I wondered how often this child had experienced this kind of interaction with her mother and other adults. Her mother seemed to shrug it off and stopped trying to get her child's attention. She took another sip of coffee and returned to her phone, her child now seemingly indifferent to her actions. A few seconds later, the mother stood up and pushed the stroller away while looking down at her phone.

As I finished my sandwich and headed off to my next meeting, the child's face kept coming to mind. I recalled that early observational attachment research noted that parents who were dismissive or intermittently available tended to have children who developed insecure patterns of attachment. It was those mothers who were good at being available and responsive to their children's requests for engagement that had children who were secure in their attachments and developed adaptive affect regulation and good attentional abilities. We now have a new and ever-present distraction that sacrifices those we are with for interactions at a distance. I can't help but wonder how devices will impact the development of our children's sense of attachment security. Could it be that a combination of screen-addicted parents and permissiveness enhances the development of insecure attachment?

Based on all that we presently know about child development, the addictive quality of the internet is doubtlessly impacting the nature of parenting, and the ability of our children to regulate their emotional lives. A central mechanism of the development of security is the consistent availability of attentive and attuned caretakers. This available attention, not just to react but also to anticipate a child's needs, is especially important early in life, when they lack the ability to self-regulate. All sorts of things occur in the environment that compete with a parent's attention and, of course, parents are not always attending to their children.

For the first time in history, a parent's environment includes ubiquitous screens that have not only been designed to capture and hold their attention, but now serve as a portal to their jobs, social life, entertainment, and their day-to-day functioning. Early in life, a child learns whether their needs will be addressed by available parents, whether the parent will arrive in response to a distress call, and whether the parent's arrival will result in reregulation or more dysregulation for the child. The infant may not have conscious thoughts about this process, but these experiences will be translated into the biochemistry and neuroanatomy of their brains. Over almost a century of research, we have learned how important our attention is to the social, emotional, and neurological development of our children.

It is vital for optimal early development that a child feels seen, felt, heard, and understood. Thus, it is important for a parent to have a higher level of executive functioning that allows them to flexibly turn their attention to the child, attune, figure out what is needed, and help the child reregulate. In addition, parents now need to have the executive abilities required to fight the addictive nature of screens.

Early attachment research shows us (and the current epigenetic research supports) that the availability of eye contact, shared gaze, reciprocal play, and the hundred other ways in which children interact with those around them stimulates their metabolism, brain growth, and learning. My best guess is that we will see an increase in depression, anxiety, and hopelessness in children if our culture and technology continue to divert parents' attention away from them. This is the usual aftermath of war, poverty, pandemics, and perhaps now, the total penetration of the internet into our moment-to-moment lives.

INNOCENT BEGINNINGS

Innocence is always unsuspicious.
JOSEPH JOUBERT

I remember the spring morning during the 1990s when I figured out how to connect a modem and found my way to AOL. I was fascinated by the new technology and sent my first emails with childish delight. I had no idea how the digital revolution would impact everything from relationships, to brain development, to how our minds process information. Between email, entertainment, and access to the news, I was hooked. I was soon able to avoid the library, get research articles, and shop for books and music online. At first, I didn't notice that the book and music stores I had spent so much time in were starting to disappear. Until recently, I likened the warnings about the internet to those of an earlier generation who warned us of the dangers of television.

Finally, I began to pay attention to the warnings. I remember having lunch at a café when I noticed a corner booth where six young women were sitting around a table—each of them looking down at their phones, actively texting and swiping away. At another table, a couple sat across from one another, both intently immersed in their phones. Months later, while working in London, I had to cross Westminster Bridge to get to work. The bridge was so packed with people taking selfies with an array of smiles and expressions, their phones on long sticks held high above their heads, that I had to be on guard for my safety. I wondered if they were really aware of where they were. Had the world become a backdrop to post images of yourself to get likes on social media? When I was their age, I carried a bulky camera to take pictures of places and scenery, statues and bridges, gardens and wildlife. But for any of these people, the photo is a selfie. It's about them in front of Big Ben, not about Big Ben, London, or the rich history surrounding them.

Closer to home, halfway through each of my classes, I say, "Okay, let's take a break." In the past, discussions would break out, and students would wander off together in search of coffee and snacks. After 10 or 15 minutes, I would have to make an effort to get most everyone's attention away from their discussions and back to the lecture. Now when I call for a break, everyone quickly reaches for their phones and sits quietly, immersed in whatever is on their screens. By the end of the break, one or two conversations may be taking place, but for the most part, most everyone has been captured by their phones. It is now even more difficult to get their attention back to the class.

Over the last few years, I have witnessed a disturbing trend in both my younger clients and my graduate students: A good number can no longer read. Of course, they know how to read, but they are unable to maintain focus long enough to get through a full paragraph of text. As they do what they call "reading," they will also be paying attention to multiple other screens, receiving and responding to messages, and sometimes even gaming. Shallow processing is adequate for superficial and fleeting content, but not for the kind of sustained focus required to understand complex concepts. High school students I work with report that it takes them eight hours to complete a one-hour assignment, and given their definition of attention and how they are "reading," it is easy to understand why. Because primary sources have become so difficult, more and more students rely on summaries and preprocessed notes, which are now also becoming too difficult to follow.

THE WAR FOR ATTENTION AND THE CRISIS OF FOCUS

Concentrate all your thoughts upon the work at hand.
The sun's rays do not burn until brought into focus.
ALEXANDER GRAHAM BELL

Advertising agencies have been fighting for our attention for the past century. They have employed psychologists and sociologists of every ilk to determine how to capture our attention and convert it into sales. Billboards, magazine ads, blimps, and telemarketers reflect the theories, research data, and best guesses of advertising wisdom. Television is a prime medium, a constantly changing billboard on which to display products. Even before the internet was launched, advertisers began to calculate its value as an advertising platform. It now employs thousands of social engineers whose sole mission is to increase the number of clicks, swipes, and minutes you rack up each day. All of these metrics are tied to advertising revenue. The internet doesn't care about your life or well-being, whether you exercise, study, sleep, eat properly, or look at your spouse or children. It only cares about income and share price. The combined crisis of insecure attachment and distractibility may be collateral damage of the internet's enormous success.

Attention is a limited resource. When we multitask, we spread our attention across a number of points—think of an air traffic controller or a waitress working 20 tables during the dinner rush. Our minds get used to constantly scanning the environment for things that might need attention, like two planes coming into the same runway or an empty glass on the table of a generous customer. On the other hand, when we focus deeply on something, we can easily miss things that are not associated with our focus—think of the absent-minded professor or an athlete who is in the zone. A professor may not notice her hunger while working on her research, or a hitter may not hear the roar of the crowd as he locks his focus on the next pitch. I think it's a safe assumption to think of attention as a limited resource that we choose to deploy in different ways across a variety of situations.

One difference between TV and the internet is that TV programs have beginnings, middles, and ends. TV parallels the stories we evolved to attend to and internalize. These stories contain central characters and a narrative arc similar to our day-to-day experience. We can certainly become habituated to television and use it to avoid the real world and regulate our fears and anxieties. But it does contain natural breaks that signal us to take back control of our own attention. Platforms like Facebook, Pinterest, and Snapchat have no starting or stopping points, no natural breaks, no morals or conclusions. They contain endless streams of content that include popups, messages, and pokes to recapture our attention if it happens to flag. The social engineers in Silicon Valley know this, counsel their local schools to be less tech dependent, and limit their own children's screen time.

UNANTICIPATED CONSEQUENCES

The Internet has compromised the quality of debate.
NOAM CHOMSKY

On the surface, people have been avoiding dealing with their problems by watching TV and going to movies for a century. A primary difference, however, is that we have become dependent on the internet to navigate life, and we carry it with us everywhere we go. The boundary between who we are and our devices has blurred in a way that is incomparable to our relationship with prior technologies. I discovered while teaching in Australia in 2019 that it was common knowledge among child therapists that some of their young clients were suffering posttraumatic stress reactions after seeing pornographic websites. A number of parents have reported to me that their kids become physically violent when devices are taken away. These are not things we have heard of related to TV or moviegoing.

In the book *iGen*, Jean Twenge (2017) has made the case that the total penetration of the internet into the lives of young children has not been positive. In reviewing the available research, she found that between 2010 and 2015, eighth, 10th, and 12th graders reported less happiness, enjoyment, and satisfaction with life, endorsing statements such as, "I can't do anything right," "I often feel left out of things," and "My life is not useful." She also reported that between 2011 and 2015, rates of depression increased, as have the suicide rates of 12- to 14-year-olds. Between 2011 and 2016, undergraduates reported increased anxiety, depression, and sleep disturbances and decreases in sleep, exercise, social engagement, and overall functioning. Dr. Twenge made the point of stressing that the usual cultural factors related to such trends, such as a bad economy and unemployment, were not present during this period.

THE ADOLESCENT BRAIN

*Adolescence is a new birth, for the higher and
more completely human traits are now born.*
G. STANLEY HALL

Why does adolescence exist? Why not just have a smooth and gradual transition from childhood to adulthood? Although I've never found a completely satisfying answer to this question, there are some good ideas about what happens to us during this time. (Having once been an adolescent myself, I suspect that my own experiences also inform my thinking.) Adolescence, the transition period from childhood to adulthood, is all about developing a broader tribal identity outside of one's immediate family. The surface goal is to be liked and accepted by peers; the deeper agenda is individuation and preparation for adult roles and responsibilities.

Over the past quarter century, it was discovered that the adolescent brain goes through a process of cortical disorganization and reorganization. In a sense, the adolescent brain is a work in progress, as is their self-identity, social relatedness, and emotional resiliency. Significant reorganization has been found to occur in the frontal lobes, corpus callosum, and cerebellum, leading to a variety of challenges such as emotional dysregulation, impaired judgment, and problems with anticipating consequences. We also see an increase in impulsive behavior, misreading and misinterpreting social cues, risk taking, and substance abuse. When negative and self-destructive behaviors occur during adolescence, the ongoing changes in adolescent brains also make it difficult to change course in a positive direction. Addictions of all kinds supercharge midbrain areas and overwhelm the cortical networks trying to develop and establish control. For all of these reasons, adolescence can be a challenging time for both the adolescent and those around them.

Throughout our evolutionary history, adolescents have worked out these challenges and built their brains through face-to-face interactions in real time. Their risk taking and trial-and-error learning have occurred in the context of social interactions in the real world. The question we now face is, how does living in a virtual world change the way our brains and minds develop and reorganize? We've evolved in tribes and go through schools with a limited number of people, many of whom we know. What happens in a virtual social space where the number of people is unlimited, social identities are highly edited, and we compare ourselves to avatars and celebrities instead of those we actually know?

During adolescence, the developing cortex allows for the consideration of distant goals and lofty ideals. It also allows for the recognition of the distance between our aspirations, objective reality, and our own capabilities. The disparity we come to recognize may inspire us to plot a course to our future or make us vulnerable to demoralization, depression, and despair. It is these negative feelings that can trigger intense internet use as an escape from both internal and external challenges, beginning a negative cycle that can include sleep deprivation, depression, anxiety, difficulties at school, lack of exercise, obesity, and social withdrawal.

DIFFERENTIAL SUSCEPTIBILITY

Four horsemen—terror, bewilderment, frustration, despair.
ALCOHOLICS ANONYMOUS

The majority of us may navigate screens just fine. We understand the forces at work, the importance of self-monitoring, and the need for a balance between our digital and analog lives. We know that our children need our attention, so we leave our phones in the car, don't take them out to dinner, and don't bring them to bed each night. When we get together with friends, we sit across from one another, sustain eye contact, and tolerate the quiet moments without reflexively reaching for our phones. We take vacations and actually engage with the scenery instead of plunging off a bridge while attempting to get the best selfie angle.

Yet there are many among us who have no such perspective or executive control. As with drugs and alcohol, there exists a differential susceptibility to addictions of all kinds based on genetics, experience, temperament, and disposition. So far, the research suggests that those with social anxiety, low self-esteem, and poor social skills are more vulnerable to internet use as a defense against their anxiety. It is easier to stay in bed and create a digital social world that they feel most comfortable with. Of course, the more they avoid actual interactions, the less skilled they become and the more anxiety they feel when they have to interact in the analog world (face-to-face). The same dynamic is also at work in those with depression or avoidant defenses who are able to avoid risking interactions, which provides immediate relief from stress but serves to deepen their symptoms and dysfunction.

The internet is certainly not all bad. For people on the autism spectrum, the elderly, those with limited physical mobility, and a range of other challenges, the internet offers a window to the world that is far more beneficial than any risk of addiction. Parents need to know their children's strengths and vulnerabilities and help them to structure wise and self-aware internet use. In discussing internet addiction, being clear about differential susceptibility will help us avoid conflating the issues of measured and pathological use. The central question may be whether you are using the internet or the internet is using you.

SCREENS IN PSYCHOTHERAPY

Clever gimmicks of mass distraction yield a cheap soul-craft of addicted and self-medicated narcissists.

CORNEL WEST

Screen use has introduced a new dynamic into the consulting room. There are adolescents and young adults who rely on having their phone in hand and become anxious and preoccupied in a session without them. There are adults whose smart watches vibrate to let them know they have a call, or their pocket erupts with buzzers, lights, and bells, or they dive into their purse to dig out their phones before the session can continue. Do we ask our clients at the beginning of session to turn off their phones, take off their smart watches, and give us their undivided attention? That is certainly one strategy, but what is the result? Deprived of their devices, are we really interacting with our clients as they are in their everyday lives, or are we creating an artificial state of mind that will become isolated to the consulting room, making it more difficult for them to generalize gains in therapy to their day-to-day lives? If our clients have incorporated their phones into how their brains and minds work, do we serve them better to build their phones into the process of psychotherapy and use them as adjuncts to treatment?

When I was in training (and this may still be true), a client who came for therapy addicted to drugs or alcohol would first be treated for their addiction before beginning psychotherapy. The thought was that their addiction would handicap their ability to be present and focused, and to benefit from outpatient treatment. It was found that specialized treatments such as inpatient detoxification, sober living companions, and 12-step programs were more successful than standard psychotherapy for addictions. If what looks like an addiction to the internet in one of its many forms—social media, gaming, pornography, gambling, and so on—is present, is it possible that the processes that lead to successful psychotherapy may be blocked in the same way? De we treat these clients as addicts who need to go through digital detox before they begin psychotherapy? These are just a few of the big questions we now face.

Whether a client is addicted to the internet or not, it has become an important point of assessment during the course of treatment. The amount of screen time may also become a reliable measure of a client's depression, anxiety, social withdrawal, and sleep disturbance. Because total internet abstinence is not a reasonable goal, addressing internet addiction will likely parallel treatment for eating disorders more than drug abuse or alcoholism. Measures are available to assess internet addiction, including the amount of use, symptoms of withdrawal, and resultant functional impairments at work and in personal relationships. Psychoeducation may go a long way to make parents and children aware of the dangers of unrestricted internet use. We face a tremendous challenge in the years to come in addressing these questions for parents, teachers, and psychotherapists—and it has only just begun.

CHAPTER 14

REFLECTIONS AND FUTURE STRATEGIES

*We find after years of struggle that we
do not take a trip; a trip takes us.*
JOHN STEINBECK

In the decades that I've been involved in clinical training, I have had the pleasure of mentoring hundreds of intelligent and compassionate individuals pursuing careers in psychology and psychotherapy. Many have become friends and colleagues with whom I continue to learn, consult, and share clients. Whenever I contemplate retirement, it is these ever-renewing connections that keep me saying, "One more year!"

Advances in neuroscience are making it clear that psychotherapy, like other forms of human relating, can be a powerful agent of change. We are learning that the nature and quality of relationships throughout life have the ability to trigger epigenetic processes that alter gene expression in ways that can heal our brains and bodies. Psychotherapy is clearly a deeply biological intervention—as well as a social, emotional, and cognitive one—that goes to the heart of the human experience. Despite what many believe, psychotherapy, when done well, has been a powerful form of healing that has made a difference in the lives of an untold number of people.

STUDENTS AS CUSTOMERS

*Selling out is doing something you don't
really want to do for money.*
BONO

This book is being published at an interesting time. As so much sophisticated knowledge about human learning and change is being accumulated, clinical training appears to be moving in the opposite direction. Driven by tuition dollars, training programs have continued to lower admission requirements, circumvent academic standards, and hire armies of inexperienced adjunct teachers. Grade inflation, lower standards, and less-prepared students are diluting the educational experience of trainees. Quality has taken such a back seat to finances that there are now entire graduate programs in psychology offered online. When students are converted into customers, the expediencies of tuition dollars override quality control, and academic excellence becomes a marketing slogan.

In an attempt at quality control, accrediting bodies continue to create ever-longer lists of academic course requirements at the cost of building clinical skills. But instead of receiving better training, students often become worn out and demoralized by jumping through countless hoops of little theoretical or practical value for the work they are supposedly being prepared for. To make matters worse, many internship sites provide inadequate supervision coupled with increasingly complex clinical cases. Having no experience or perspective, students naturally believe that this is how training works. Students often tell me they feel as if they are flying by the seat of their pants in the consulting room. They are left feeling that their inadequacies are their fault and come to feel like imposters. One student told me, "I go into each session hoping my client has a lot to say, because if they stop talking,

I have no idea what to do." Even worse for me is listening to fragmented case presentations. When I ask the student, "What did your supervisor say?," they tell me that they often receive little to no guidance. To say that these developments make me both sad and disillusioned would be a gross understatement. I regret the lost opportunities for young clinicians to obtain the supervision and mentorship I was privileged to receive in my training.

Although I know that there are excellent supervisors who are dedicated to teaching and clinical practice, based on the feedback from my students, they are not in the majority. Put it all together, and many leave training faking it and calling whatever they have pieced together "psychotherapy." Even after years of training, many come to rely on the tactics and strategies they discover in the self-help books they happen to run across. The field's dirty little secret is that a degree and a license are often unrelated to competence. If the system has turned students into customers, then many aren't getting what they paid for. If a client assumes that the degree on the therapist's wall means that they are qualified, all I can say is caveat emptor.

STUDENTS AS CLIENTS

We make no apologies for setting high standards.
NANCY ZIMPHER

For these reasons and more, too many students graduate from training programs who should never have been allowed to see clients. A few lack the cognitive skills and executive abilities to handle the rigors of graduate school, let alone the challenges of a clinical practice. For others, characterological issues and unresolved trauma block their ability to learn and greatly limit their abilities and self-awareness.

The challenges faced by these troubled students are much the same as in those seeking therapy. In response, academic administrators come to treat them as clients. They are compassionate and understanding of their limitations, personality flaws, and trauma-based incapacities. They counsel them, spend extra time doing therapy in their offices, and become their champions when other faculty bring up problems with their work. Treating students as clients may be an occupational hazard for psychotherapists that leads some to be unable to offer the clear (and sometimes difficult) feedback they need to hear.

Christina Rummell (2015) surveyed 119 doctoral-level clinical and counseling students in APA-accredited programs about their physical and psychological health and well-being. Results of her survey indicated that 49% reported clinically significant anxiety symptoms; 39% reported clinically significant depressive symptoms; and 34% reported clinically significant symptoms of both. More than half also reported chronic physical health symptoms that increased with greater workload. Many students reported inadequate support from supervisors and limited use of ancillary counseling. The broad needs of these students, ironically surrounded by mental health professionals, are being mostly missed. Faculty may be treating their students like clients by adjusting program requirements to fit their capabilities, but they are not making available the psychological help they need.

I believe that in order to do therapy, we need to be engaged in therapy and brutally honest with ourselves, not only for our own development but for the welfare of our clients. I believe that the standards should be high, that not everyone is cut out to be a therapist, and it is a training program's responsibility to deselect those students who, based on our judgment as psychologists, are unfit to serve as such. We are presumed to be serving as gatekeepers for the profession but pass that responsibility to the supervisors, who pass it on to the licensing agencies, who now pass it on to the consumer—in reality, no one is paying attention. Somewhere along the line, we abdicated our responsibility to protect the public from people that we feel shouldn't be therapists. What I've heard instead is the constant mantra of "go along to get along."

What has gotten lost in all of this is something that seemed very important when I was a student—the duty to protect the public. While often a topic in the classes I teach, I don't think I've ever heard it mentioned in a faculty meeting. Over the years I have heard from administrators that "we need the numbers," "we don't want to get sued," "the student has rights," "they've invested so much in their education," "hopefully they won't make it through their practicum," and my favorite, "not all clients need to be seen by excellent therapists." Nothing about protecting the public or how we need to uphold higher standards.

TAKING CONTROL OF YOUR TRAINING

When making your choice in life, do not neglect to live.
SAMUEL JOHNSON

Why is any of this relevant to those in the early stages of their career? The take-home message from all of these unfortunate professional developments means that **the quality of our education, training, and clinical work is entirely up to us.** While to some degree this has always been the case, it has never been as true as it is today. Going through a graduate program, getting straight As, and getting licensed does not necessarily mean you are ready to see clients. Don't be fooled by those selling degrees and certifications that you have all you need to become a competent therapist.

At this point, it is up to you to begin the lifelong process of exploration and growth by creating a team of supervisors, teachers, mentors, and colleagues who you can continue to learn from and who challenge your limits. When choosing a supervisor, it is important to be a wise and informed consumer. Make sure you interview a number of potential supervisors, read the papers they have written, attend their lectures, and get a good sense of whether they can serve the next steps of your development. You want to be challenged by new ideas, theories, and practice techniques that stretch your current skills and abilities. While it's important, a good connection with your supervisor is a necessary but not sufficient condition for successful supervision. The important thing is to receive honest feedback concerning areas which require further development in a constructive, competence-inspiring, and ideally kind manner.

Training in psychotherapy can lead to a variety of career choices, including mental health, the military, the justice system, and community, industrial, and educational settings. There is an array of degrees, job opportunities, and career choices. One of the problems in making a choice is that a lot of vital information only comes after you pursue a path. It takes heart to stay on a path; it also takes heart and courage to change paths if you come to realize you have chosen one that is not right for you.

Gone are the years of curiosity that marked my generation—the permission to take your time, go on a walkabout, and find your inspiration. The joys and anxieties of exploration seem to have been replaced by the pressure of having a clearly defined path by the junior year of high school. Many feel they should have their life charted out before they have the chance to experience any of it. I find this to be a great tragedy that may be contributing to the rise of anxiety and depression in adolescents and young adults. There is danger in not making positive use of the uncertainty of the stage of life between childhood and adulthood. I have found that those who do not engage in this journey search for external answers to internal challenges. The acceptance of a socially prescribed path is no substitute for self-exploration, personal growth, and choices that can only come from the heart.

PASSION LEADS TO PURPOSE

My general formula for my students is "Follow your bliss."
Find where it is, and don't be afraid to follow it.
JOSEPH CAMPBELL

Doing the right thing only gets you so far. As Freud said, when it comes to important decisions, you have to consult your intuition, your unconscious, and your heart. To paraphrase Thoreau, choosing an ill-fitting path to avoid the anxiety of uncertainty can lead to a life of quiet desperation. It is important to realize, up front, that settling for a career and a life that are not a good fit will have a high cost. And while it may seem that you are behind your time in making a career choice, it is not something to rush into just to avoid the anxiety of uncertainty.

When I was 12, my family moved to an apartment across the street from a baseball field. Annoyed by seeing me sitting in front of the TV, my mother banished me from the apartment with the command "Go play!" As a shy, chubby, and uncoordinated kid, going through the gate onto the ballfield felt like entering purgatory. But there I was. My new and very stiff glove on my left hand, I slowly walked down the foul line to assess the situation. It wasn't long before a group of boys, already on the field, asked me to fill a gap in the outfield. Everyone soon realized I was a terrible outfielder. I wasn't able to catch the balls that came my way, but I could run them down and throw them back into the infield. This was improvement enough over having to fetch the balls themselves to allow me to keep playing.

Something important happened inside me on that day. I became interested in baseball; the geometry of batting, the stance of the hitter, the relative speed of pitch and swing. I wanted to learn how to predict where the ball would be hit. I went back down to the field the next day, curious to test my ideas from the day before, and found I was slightly better at placing myself in the outfield and getting to where the ball was hit. Learning to actually catch it was another thing altogether. I was heartened by my successes and became obsessed with the game. After that, I couldn't change my clothes fast enough when I got home from school to get down to the field. My mother felt like a brilliant parent for having banished me from the apartment, although she now complained that she hardly ever saw me.

A dozen years later, while I was a graduate student, I was in a class called physiological psychology, where we studied the brain and participated in laboratory experiments. As part of this class I had to read a collection of articles that described the effects of brain damage on learning and behavior in rats. At first this seemed like torture, but to my surprise, I became fascinated by the implications of this research for understanding human experience—the core interest in my studies of theology. As in my experience with baseball, I became insatiable for more knowledge, and found myself distracted from my other classes. I made it a goal to read whatever I could, which, in those days, wasn't that much. It turns out that my passion for learning about neuroscience has continued, unabated, for over 40 years. While studying neuroscience made no logical sense at the time, it eventually became a central part of my life and work. These two lessons taught me that trusting my instincts and following my heart have usually paid off in one way or another.

Ironically, the ability to be sensitive to my instincts and follow my heart required a kind of surrender. I had to surrender to my own brokenness, learn to care for myself, and trust my decisions, even when I couldn't explain or justify them to the satisfaction of others. I had to find a way to be still enough to be able to hear the inner voices that were trying to help me navigate my life. When I tried to hide my vulnerabilities, I put on an act and stopped listening to my heart. I risked pursuing paths that might impress or appease, but weren't a good fit for me. My advice is to learn to pay attention to the subtle messages from your heart and follow them. Just as important, know that the voices in your head will criticize your choices in order to keep you on the path that others would prefer. It is important to channel your inner alpha and learn to tell these voices to "Shut the #%!? up."

Ultimately, only you know what's right for you, so you have to build a good enough relationship with yourself to be able to find the answers to these questions. The goal is to discover something that you look forward to doing when you get out of bed each morning, something you naturally turn toward, as a flower turns toward the sun. Explore, be open, be willing to fail, and don't take another person's word for who you are. If you are to build a meaningful career as a psychotherapist, you have to learn, first and foremost, how to silence your mind, listen to your heart, and pursue knowledge.

REFERENCES AND
SUGGESTED READINGS

Cozolino, L. (2004). *The making of a therapist.* New York: Norton.

Cozolino, L. (2014). *The neuroscience of human relationships.* New York: Norton.

Cozolino, L. (2016). *Why therapy works.* New York: Norton.

Dana, D. (2018). *The polyvagal theory in therapy.* New York: Norton.

Kahneman, D. (2011). *Thinking, fast and slow.* New York: Farrar, Straus and Giroux.

Lewis, M. (2017). *The undoing project.* New York: Norton.

Oliver, M. (1999). *Winter hours.* Boston: Houghton Mifflin.

Porges, S. (2011). *The polyvagal theory.* New York: Norton.

Reich, W. (1945). *Character analysis.* New York: Touchstone.

Reik, T. (1948). *Listening with the third ear: The inner experience of a psychoanalyst.* New York: Farrar, Straus and Giroux.

Rogers, C. (1961). *On becoming a person.* Boston: Houghton Mifflin.

Rummel, C (2015). An exploratory study of psychology graduate student workload, health, and program satisfaction. *Professional psychology: Research and practice. 46*(6), 391–399.

Sharaf, M. R. (1983). *Fury on earth: A biography of Wilhelm Reich.* New York: St. Martin's.

Twenge, J. M. (2017). *iGen: Why today's super-connected kids are growing up less rebellious, more tolerant, less happy and completely unprepared for adulthood.* New York: Simon and Schuster.

Zhou, Y., Lin, F., Du, Y., Qin, L., Zhao, Z., Xu, J. & Lei, H. (2011). Gray matter abnormalities in Internet addiction: A voxel-based morphometry study. *European Journal of Radiology, 79,* 92–95.

INDEX